Filters and Freedom

Free Speech Perspectives on Internet Content Controls

Electronic Privacy Information Center
Washington, DC

About the Electronic Privacy Information Center

The Electronic Privacy Information Center (EPIC) is a public interest research center in Washington, D.C. It was established in 1994 to focus public attention on emerging civil liberties issues and to protect privacy, the First Amendment, and constitutional values. EPIC is a project of the Fund for Constitutional Government. EPIC works in association with Privacy International, an international human rights group based in London, UK and is also a member of the Global Internet Liberty Campaign, the Internet Free Expression Alliance and the Internet Privacy Coalition.

The EPIC Bookstore provides a comprehensive selection of books and reports on computer security, cryptography, the First Amendment and free speech, open government, and privacy. Visit the EPIC Bookstore at www.epic.org/bookstore/.

EPIC Staff

Marc Rotenberg, Executive Director
David L. Sobel, General Counsel
Andrew Shen, Policy Analyst
David Banisar, Senior Fellow
Wayne Madsen, Senior Fellow
Dori Kornfeld, Policy Fellow
Ethan Preston, Law Clerk

Acknowledgments

The Electronic Privacy Information Center gratefully acknowledges the many individuals and organizations, particularly the members of the Internet Free Expression Alliance (IFEA) and the Global Internet Liberty Campaign (GILC), who have drawn attention to the problems associated with content controls and the need to ensure that freedom of expression is preserved in the online world. We also appreciate the work of the following foundations that are supporting efforts to protect free speech: the EPIC Trust, the Fund for Constitutional Government, the HKH Foundation, the List Foundation, the Open Society Institute, and the Scherman Foundation.

Preface

The foibles of filters are now well-known. Several thoughtful critiques and studies have been produced since filtering and rating systems were first proposed as voluntary alternatives to government regulation of Internet content. Originally touted as a technological panacea that would ward off the evils of official censorship, filtering has been shown to pose its own significant threats to free expression in new communications media. Once characterized by their proponents as mere "features" or "tools," filtering and rating systems are now viewed more realistically as fundamental architectural changes that may, in fact, facilitate the suppression of speech far more effectively than national laws alone ever could.

The international human rights and free expression communities have been in the forefront of sounding the alarms and fostering more deliberate consideration of so-called "self-regulatory" approaches to Internet content control. The Global Internet Liberty Campaign (www.gilc.org) has monitored the development of filtering proposals around the world. In the United States, the Internet Free Expression Alliance (www.ifea.net) has been an important voice in the national debate on content regulation, identifying new threats to free expression and First Amendment values on the Internet, whether legal or technological. The members of these coalitions have produced the ground-breaking papers and reports that are contained in this collection.

In "Fahrenheit 451.2: Is Cyberspace Burning?," the American Civil Liberties Union warns that, "government and industry leaders alike are now inching toward the dangerous and incorrect position that the Internet is like television, and should be rated and censored accordingly." The principal technical standard for rating and filtering content – the Platform for Internet Content Selection – is critiqued by Irene Graham of Electronic Frontiers Australia in "Will PICS Torch Free Speech on the Internet?" In "Sites Censored by Censorship Software," Peacefire shows how software filters block access to many educational, medical, and political resources. A British perspective on Internet content controls is presented in "Who Watches the Watchmen: Internet Content Rating Systems, and Privatised Censorship," a report prepared by Cyber-Rights & Cyber-Liberties (UK).

The theoretical benefits of filtering systems have been undercut by hands-on testing that demonstrates the actual (and troubling) impact of these techniques. Two such studies are included here. The Electronic Privacy Information Center's "Faulty Filters: How Content Filters Block Access to Kid-Friendly Information on the Internet," was one of the first reports that documented the potential damage to free expression that can result from a ratings regime. More recently, the Censorware Project examined the real-world impact of a filtering system in "Censored Internet Access in Utah Public Schools and Libraries." These reports present important findings that filtering proponents must address. In its "Filtering FAQ," Computer Professionals for Social Responsibility provides detailed answers to commonly asked question about software filters.

The global nature of the Internet requires multinational participation in the development of standards and policies that could irreparably alter the Internet's potential to facilitate freedom of expression. The Global Internet Liberty Campaign (GILC) has adopted as a founding principle that "on-line free expression not be restricted by indirect means such as excessively restrictive governmental or private controls over computer hardware or software, telecommunications infrastructure, or other essential components of the Internet." Two GILC statements – "Impact of Self-Regulation and Filtering on Human Rights to Freedom of Expression" and its "Submission to the World Wide Web Consortium on PICSRules" – reflect the international concern over "voluntary" proposals to control on-line content.

Libraries increasingly are becoming battlegrounds in the debate over Internet filtering. The American Civil Liberties Union's "Censorship in a Box: Why Blocking Software is Wrong for Public Libraries" demonstrates how all blocking software censors valuable speech and gives librarians, educators and parents a false sense of security when providing minors with Internet access. In "The Cyber-Library: Legal and Policy Issues Facing Public Libraries in the High-Tech Era," the National Coalition Against Censorship addresses efforts to censor Internet use in libraries, examines some of the concerns raised by censorship advocates and summarizes libraries' responses to these efforts.

Partly as a result of these writings, the headlong rush toward the development and acceptance of filtering and rating systems has slowed. From a free speech perspective, thoughtful consideration of these initiatives is clearly desirable. Although generally well-intentioned, proposals for "self-regulation" of Internet content carry with them a substantial risk of limiting free expression and damaging the medium in unintended ways. The views expressed in this collection must be considered carefully if we are to prevent such an outcome.

> David L. Sobel
> September 1999
> Washington, DC

Table of Contents

Table of Contents

Fahrenheit 451.2: Is Cyberspace Burning? How Rating and Blocking Proposals May Torch Free Speech on the Internet

American Civil Liberties Union

Executive Summary

In the landmark case *Reno v. ACLU*, the Supreme Court overturned the Communications Decency Act, declaring that the Internet deserves the same high level of free speech protection afforded to books and other printed matter.

But today, all that we have achieved may now be lost, if not in the bright flames of censorship then in the dense smoke of the many ratings and blocking schemes promoted by some of the very people who fought for freedom.

The ACLU and others in the cyber-liberties community were genuinely alarmed by the tenor of a recent White House summit meeting on Internet censorship at which industry leaders pledged to create a variety of schemes to regulate and block controversial online speech.

But it was not any one proposal or announcement that caused our alarm; rather, it was the failure to examine the longer-term implications for the Internet of rating and blocking schemes.

The White House meeting was clearly the first step away from the principle that protection of the electronic word is analogous to protection of the printed word. Despite the Supreme Court's strong rejection of a broadcast analogy for the Internet, government and industry leaders alike are now inching toward the

---

dangerous and incorrect position that the Internet is like television, and should be rated and censored accordingly.

Is Cyberspace burning? Not yet, perhaps. But where there's smoke, there's fire.

> "Any content-based regulation of the Internet, no matter how benign the purpose, could burn the global village to roast the pig."
>
> U.S. Supreme Court majority decision, *Reno v. ACLU* (June 26, 1997)

Introduction

In his chilling (and prescient) novel about censorship, Fahrenheit 451, author Ray Bradbury describes a futuristic society where books are outlawed. "Fahrenheit 451" is, of course, the temperature at which books burn.

In Bradbury's novel – and in the physical world – people censor the printed word by burning books. But in the virtual world, one can just as easily censor controversial speech by banishing it to the farthest corners of cyberspace using rating and blocking programs. Today, will Fahrenheit, version 451.2 – a new kind of virtual censorship – be the temperature at which cyberspace goes up in smoke?

The first flames of Internet censorship appeared two years ago, with the introduction of the Federal Communications Decency Act (CDA), outlawing "indecent" online speech. But in the landmark case *Reno v. ACLU*, the Supreme Court overturned the CDA, declaring that the Internet is entitled to the highest level of free speech protection. In other words, the Court said that online speech deserved the protection afforded to books and other printed matter.

Today, all that we have achieved may now be lost, if not in the bright flames of censorship then in the dense smoke of the many ratings and blocking schemes promoted by some of the very people who fought for freedom. And in the end, we may find that the censors have indeed succeeded in "burning down the house to roast the pig."

Is Cyberspace Burning?

The ashes of the CDA were barely smoldering when the White House called a summit meeting to encourage Internet users to self-rate their speech and to urge industry leaders to develop and deploy the tools for blocking "inappropriate" speech. The meeting was "voluntary," of course: the White House claimed it wasn't holding anyone's feet to the fire.

The ACLU and others in the cyber-liberties community were genuinely alarmed by the tenor of the White House summit and the unabashed enthusiasm for technological fixes that will make it easier to block or render invisible controversial speech. (Note: see appendix for detailed explanations of the various technologies.)

Industry leaders responded to the White House call with a barrage of announcements:

- Netscape announced plans to join Microsoft – together the two giants have 90% or more of the web browser market – in adopting PICS (Platform for Internet Content Selection) the rating standard that establishes a consistent way to rate and block online content;

- IBM announced it was making a $100,000 grant to RSAC (Recreational Software Advisory Council) to encourage the use of its RSACi rating system. Microsoft Explorer already employs the RSACi ratings system, Compuserve encourages its use and it is fast becoming the de facto industry standard rating system;

- Four of the major search engines – the services which allow users to conduct searches of the Internet for relevant sites – announced a plan to cooperate in the promotion of "self-regulation" of the Internet. The president of one, Lycos, was quoted in a news account as having "thrown down the gauntlet" to the other three, challenging them to agree to exclude unrated sites from search results;

- Following announcement of proposed legislation by Sen. Patty Murray (D Wash.), which would impose civil and ultimately criminal penalties on those who mis-rate a site, the makers of the blocking program Safe Surf proposed similar legislation, the "Online Cooperative Publishing Act."

But it was not any one proposal or announcement that caused our alarm; rather, it was the failure to examine the longer-term implications for the Internet of rating and blocking schemes.

What may be the result? The Internet will become bland and homogenized. The major commercial sites will still be readily available they will have the resources and inclination to self-rate, and third-party rating services will be inclined to give them acceptable ratings. People who disseminate quirky and idiosyncratic speech, create individual home pages, or post to controversial news groups, will be among the first Internet users blocked by filters and made invisible by the search engines. Controversial speech will still exist, but will only be visible to those with the tools and know-how to penetrate the dense smokescreen of industry "self-regulation."

As bad as this very real prospect is, it can get worse. Faced with the reality that, although harder to reach, sex, hate speech and other controversial matter is still available on the Internet, how long will it be before governments begin to make use of an Internet already configured to accommodate massive censorship? If you look at these various proposals in a larger context, a very plausible scenario emerges. It is a scenario which in some respects has already been set in motion:

- First, the use of PICS becomes universal; providing a uniform method for content rating.

- Next, one or two rating systems dominate the market and become the de facto standard for the Internet.

- PICS and the dominant rating(s) system are built into Internet software as an automatic default.

- Unrated speech on the Internet is effectively blocked by these defaults.

- Search engines refuse to report on the existence of unrated or "unacceptably" rated sites.

- Governments frustrated by "indecency" still on the Internet make self-rating mandatory and mis-rating a crime.

The scenario is, for now, theoretical – but inevitable. It is clear that any scheme that allows access to unrated speech will fall afoul of the government-coerced push for a "family friendly" Internet. We are moving inexorably toward a system that blocks speech simply because it is unrated and makes criminals of those who mis-rate.

The White House meeting was clearly the first step in that direction and away from the principle that protection of the electronic word is analogous to protection of the printed word. Despite the Supreme Court's strong rejection of a broadcast analogy for the Internet, government and industry leaders alike are now inching toward the dangerous and incorrect position that the Internet is like television, and should berated and censored accordingly.

Is Cyberspace burning? Not yet, perhaps. But where there's smoke, there's fire.

Free Speech Online: A Victory Under Siege

On June 26, 1997, the Supreme Court held in *Reno v. ACLU* that the Communications Decency Act, which would have made it a crime to communicate anything "indecent" on the Internet, violated the First Amendment. It was the nature of the Internet itself, and the quality of speech on the Internet, that led the Court to declare that the Internet is entitled to the same broad free speech protections given to books, magazines, and casual conversation.

The ACLU argued, and the Supreme Court agreed, that the CDA was unconstitutional because, although aimed at protecting minors, it effectively banned speech among adults. Similarly, many of the rating and blocking proposals, though designed to limit minors' access, will inevitably restrict the ability of adults to communicate on the Internet. In addition, such proposals will restrict the rights of older minors to gain access to material that clearly has value for them.

Rethinking the Rush to Rate

This paper examines the free speech implications of the various proposals for Internet blocking and rating. Individually, each of the proposals poses some threat to open and robust speech on the Internet; some pose a considerably greater threat than others.

Even more ominous is the fact that the various schemes for rating and blocking, taken together, could create a black cloud of private "voluntary" censorship that is every bit as threatening as the CDA itself to what the Supreme Court called "the most participatory form of mass speech yet developed."

We call on industry leaders, Internet users, policy makers and parents groups to engage in a genuine debate about the free speech ramifications of the rating and blocking schemes being proposed.

To open the door to a meaningful discussion, we offer the following recommendations and principles:

Recommendations and Principles

- Internet users know best. The primary responsibility for determining what speech to access should remain with the individual Internet user; parents should take primary responsibility for determining what their children should access.

- Default setting on free speech. Industry should not develop products that require speakers to rate their own speech or be blocked by default.

- Buyers beware. The producers of user-based software programs should make their lists of blocked speech available to consumers. The industry should develop products that provide maximum user control.

- No government coercion or censorship. The First Amendment prevents the government from imposing, or from coercing industry into imposing, a mandatory Internet ratings scheme.

- Libraries are free speech zones. The First Amendment prevents the government, including public libraries, from mandating the use of user-based blocking software.

Six Reasons Why Self-Rating Schemes Are Wrong for the Internet

To begin with, the notion that citizens should "self-rate" their speech is contrary to the entire history of free speech in America. A proposal that we rate our online speech is no less offensive to the First Amendment than a proposal that publishers of books and magazines rate each and every article or story, or a proposal that everyone engaged in a street corner conversation rate his or her comments. But that is exactly what will happen to books, magazines, and any kind of speech that appears online under a self-rating scheme.

In order to illustrate the very practical consequences of these schemes, consider the following six reasons, and their accompanying examples, illustrating why the ACLU is against self-rating:

Reason #1: Self-Rating Schemes Will Cause Controversial Speech To Be Censored.

Kiyoshi Kuromiya, founder and sole operator of Critical Path Aids Project, has a web site that includes safer sex information written in street language with explicit diagrams, in order to reach the widest possible audience. Kuromiya doesn't want to apply the rating "crude" or "explicit" to his speech, but if he doesn't, his site will be blocked as an unrated site. If he does rate, his speech will be lumped in with "pornography" and blocked from view. Under either choice, Kuromiya has been effectively blocked from reaching a large portion of his intended audience – teenage Internet users – as well as adults.

As this example shows, the consequences of rating are far from neutral. The ratings themselves are all pejorative by definition, and they result in certain speech being blocked.

The White House has compared Internet ratings to "food labels" – but that analogy is simply wrong. Food labels provide objective, scientifically verifiable information to help the consumer make choices about what to buy, e.g. the percentage of fat in a food product like milk. Internet ratings are subjective value judgments that result in certain speech being blocked to many viewers. Further, food labels are placed on products that are readily available to consumers – unlike Internet labels, which would place certain kinds of speech out of reach of Internet users.

What is most critical to this issue is that speech like Kuromiya's is entitled to the highest degree of Constitutional protection. This is why ratings requirements have never been imposed on those who speak via the printed word. Kuromiya could distribute the same material in print form on any street corner or in any bookstore without worrying about having to rate it. In fact, a number of Supreme Court cases have established that the First Amendment does not allow government to compel speakers to say something they don't want to say – and that includes pejorative ratings. There is simply no justification for treating the Internet any differently.

Reason #2: Self-Rating Is Burdensome, Unwieldy, and Costly.

Art on the Net is a large, non-profit web site that hosts online "studios" where hundreds of artists display their work. The vast majority of the artwork has no sexual content, although there's an occasional Rubenesque painting. The ratings systems don't make sense when applied to art. Yet Art on the Net would still have to review and apply a rating to the more than 26,000 pages on its site, which would require time and staff that they just don't have. Or, they would have to require the artists themselves to self-rate, an option they find objectionable. If they decline to rate, they will be blocked as an unrated site even though most Internet users would hardly object to the art reaching minors, let alone adults.

As the Supreme Court noted in *Reno v. ACLU*, one of the virtues of the Internet is that it provides "relatively unlimited, low-cost capacity for communication of all kinds." In striking down the CDA, the Court held that imposing age-verification costs on Internet speakers would be "prohibitively expensive for noncommercial – as well as some commercial – speakers." Similarly, the burdensome requirement of self-rating thousands of pages of information would effectively shut most noncommercial speakers out of the Internet marketplace.

The technology of embedding the rating is also far from trivial. In a winning ACLU case that challenged a New York state online censorship statute, *ALA v. Pataki*, one long-time Internet expert testified that he tried to embed an RSACi label in his online newsletter site but finally gave up after several hours.

In addition, the ratings systems are simply unequipped to deal with the diversity of content now available on the Internet. There is perhaps nothing as subjective as a viewer's reaction to art. As history has shown again and again, one woman's masterpiece is another woman's pornography. How can ratings such as "explicit" or "crude" be used to categorize art? Even ratings systems that try to take artistic value into account will be inherently subjective, especially when applied by artists themselves, who will naturally consider their own work to have merit.

The variety of news-related sites on the Web will be equally difficult to rate. Should explicit war footage be labeled "violent" and blocked from view to teenagers? If along news article has one curse word, is the curse word rated individually, or is the entire story rated and then blocked?

Even those who propose that "legitimate" news organizations should not be required to rate their sites stumble over the question of who will decide what is legitimate news.

Reason #3: Conversation Can't Be Rated.

You are in a chat room or a discussion group – one of the thousands of conversational areas of the Net. A victim of sexual abuse has posted a plea for help, and you want to respond. You've heard about a variety of ratings systems, but you've never used one. You read the RSACi web page, but you can't figure out how to rate the discussion of sex and violence in your response. Aware of the penalties for mis-labeling, you decide not to send your message after all. The burdens of self-rating really hit home when applied to the vibrant, conversational areas of the Internet. Most Internet users don't run web pages, but millions of people around the world send messages, short and long, every day, to chat rooms, news groups and mailing lists. A rating requirement for these areas of the Internet would be analogous to requiring all of us to rate our telephone or streetcorner or dinner party or water cooler conversations.

The only other way to rate these areas of cyberspace would be to rate entire chatrooms or news groups rather than individual messages. But most discussion groups aren't controlled by a specific person, so who would be responsible for rating them? In addition, discussion groups that contain some objectionable material would likely also have a wide variety of speech totally appropriate and valuable for minors – but the entire forum would be blocked from view for everyone.

Reason #4: Self-Rating Will Create "Fortress America" on the Internet.

You are a native of Papua, New Guinea, and as an anthropologist you have published several papers about your native culture. You create a web site and post electronic versions of your papers, in order to share them with colleagues and other interested people around the world. You haven't heard about the move in America to rate Internet content. You don't know it, but since your site is unrated none of your colleagues in America will be able to access it.

People from all corners of the globe – people who might otherwise never connect because of their vast geographical differences – can now communicate on the Internet both easily and cheaply. One of the most dangerous aspects of ratings systems is their potential to build borders around American- and foreign-created speech. It is important to remember that today, nearly half of all Internet speech originates from outside the United States.

Even if powerful American industry leaders coerced other countries into adopting American ratings systems, how would these ratings make any sense to a New Guinean? Imagine that one of the anthropology papers explicitly describes a ritual in which teenage boys engage in self-mutilation as part of a rite of passage in achieving manhood. Would you look at it through the eyes of an American and rate it "torture," or would you rate it "appropriate for minors" for the New Guinea audience?

Reason #5: Self-Ratings Will Only Encourage, Not Prevent, Government Regulation.

The webmaster for Betty's Smut Shack, a web site that sells sexually explicit photos, learns that many people won't get to his site if he either rates his site "sexually explicit" or fails to rate at all. He rates his entire web site "okay for minors." A powerful Congressman from the Midwest learns that the site is now available to minors. He is outraged, and quickly introduces a bill imposing criminal penalties for mis-rated sites.

Without a penalty system for mis-rating, the entire concept of a self-ratings system breaks down. The Supreme Court that decided *Reno v. ACLU* would probably agree that the statute theorized above would violate the First Amendment, but as we saw with the CDA, that won't necessarily prevent lawmakers from passing it.

In fact, as noted earlier, a senator from Washington state (home of industry giant Microsoft, among others) has already proposed a law that creates criminal penalties for mis-rating. Not to be outdone, the filtering software company Safe Surf has proposed the introduction of a virtually identical federal law, including a provision that allows parents to sue speakers for damages if they "negligently" mis-rate their speech.

The example above shows that, despite all good intentions, the application of ratings systems is likely to lead to heavy-handed government censorship. Moreover, the targets of that censorship are likely to be just the sort of relatively powerless and controversial speakers, like the groups Critical Path Aids Project, Stop Prisoner Rape, Planned Parenthood, Human Rights Watch, and the various gay and lesbian organizations we represented in *Reno v. ACLU*.

Reason #6: Self-Ratings Schemes Will Turn the Internet into a Homogenized Medium Dominated by Commercial Speakers.

Huge entertainment conglomerates, such as the Disney Corporation or Time Warner, consult their platoons of lawyers who advise that their web sites must be rated to reach the widest possible audience. They then hire and train staff to rate all of their web pages. Everybody in the world will have access to their speech.

There is no question that there may be some speakers on the Internet for whom the ratings systems will impose only minimal burdens: the large, powerful corporate speakers with the money to hire legal counsel and staff to apply the necessary ratings. The commercial side of the Net continues to grow, but so far the democratic nature of the Internet has put commercial speakers on equal footing with all of the other non-commercial and individual speakers.

Today, it is just as easy to find the Critical Path AIDS web site as it is to find the Disney site. Both speakers are able to reach a worldwide audience. But mandatory Internet self-rating could easily turn the most participatory communications medium the world has yet seen into a bland, homogenized, medium dominated by powerful American corporate speakers.

Is Third-Party Rating the Answer?

Third-party ratings systems, designed to work in tandem with PICS labeling, have been held out by some as the answer to the free speech problems posed by self-rating schemes. On the plus side, some argue, ratings by an independent third party could minimize the burden of self-rating on speakers and could reduce the inaccuracy and mis-rating problems of self-rating. In fact, one of the touted strengths of the original PICS proposal was that a variety of third-party ratings systems would develop and users could pick and choose from the system that best fit their values. But third party ratings systems still pose serious free speech concerns.

First, a multiplicity of ratings systems has not yet emerged on the market, probably due to the difficulty of any one company or organization trying to rate over a million web sites, with hundreds of new sites – not to mention discussion groups and chat rooms – springing up daily.

Second, under third-party rating systems, unrated sites still may be blocked.

When choosing which sites to rate first, it is likely that third-party raters will rate the most popular web sites first, marginalizing individual and non-commercial sites. And like the self-rating systems, third-party ratings will apply subjective and value-laden ratings that could result in valuable material being blocked to adults and older minors. In addition, available third-party rating systems have no notification procedure, so speakers have no way of knowing whether their speech has received a negative rating.

The fewer the third-party ratings products available, the greater the potential for arbitrary censorship. Powerful industry forces may lead one product to dominate the marketplace. If, for example, virtually all households use Microsoft Internet Explorer and Netscape, and the browsers, in turn, use RSACi as their system, RSACi could become the default censorship system for the Internet. In addition, federal and state governments could pass laws mandating use of a particular ratings system in schools or libraries. Either of these scenarios could devastate the diversity of the Internet marketplace.

Pro-censorship groups have argued that a third-party rating system for the Internet is no different from the voluntary Motion Picture Association of America ratings for movies that we've all lived with for years. But there is an important distinction: only a finite number of movies are produced in a given year. In contrast, the amount of content on the Internet is infinite. Movies are a static, definable product created by a small number of producers; speech on the Internet is seamless, interactive, and conversational. MPAA ratings also don't come with automatic blocking mechanisms.

The Problems with User-Based Blocking Software in the Home

With the explosive growth of the Internet, and in the wake of the recent censorship battles, the marketplace has responded with a wide variety of user-based blocking programs. Each company touts the speed and efficiency of its staff members in blocking speech that they have determined is inappropriate for minors. The programs also often block speech based on keywords. (This can result in sites such as www.middlesex.gov or www.SuperBowlXXX.com being blocked because they contain the keywords "sex" and "XXX.")

In *Reno v. ACLU*, the ACLU successfully argued that the CDA violated the First Amendment because it was not the least restrictive means of addressing the government's asserted interest in protecting children from inappropriate material. In supporting this argument, we suggested that a less restrictive alternative was the availability of user-based blocking programs, e.g. Net Nanny, that parents could use in the home if they wished to limit their child's Internet access.

While user-based blocking programs present troubling free speech concerns, we still believe today that they are far preferable to any statute that imposes criminal penalties on online speech. In contrast, many of the new ratings schemes pose far greater free speech concerns than do user-based software programs.

Each user installs the program on her home computer and turns the blocking mechanism on or off at will. The programs do not generally block sites that they haven't rated, which means that they are not 100 percent effective.

Unlike the third-party ratings or self-rating schemes, these products usually do not work in concert with browsers and search engines, so the home user rather than an outside company sets the defaults. (However, it should be noted that this "standalone" feature could theoretically work against free speech principles, since here, too, it would be relatively easy to draft a law mandating the use of the products, under threat of criminal penalties.)

While the use of these products avoids some of the larger control issues with ratings systems, the blocking programs are far from problem-free. A number of products have been shown to block access to a wide variety of information that many would consider appropriate for minors. For example, some block access to safer sex information, although the Supreme Court has held that teenagers have the right to obtain access to such information even without their parent's consent. Other products block access to information of interest to the gay and lesbian community. Some products even block speech simply because it criticizes their product.

Some products allow home users to add or subtract particular sites from a list of blocked sites. For example, a parent can decide to allow access to "playboy.com" by removing it from the blocked sites list, and can deny access to "powerrangers.com" by adding it to the list. However most products consider their lists of blocked speech to be proprietary information which they will not disclose.

Despite these problems, the use of blocking programs has been enthusiastically and uncritically endorsed by government and industry leaders alike. At the recent White House summit, Vice President Gore, along with industry and non-profit groups, announced the creation of www.netparents.org, a site that provides direct links to a variety of blocking programs.

The ACLU urges the producers of all of these products to put real power in users' hands and provide full disclosure of their list of blocked speech and the criteria for blocking.

In addition, the ACLU urges the industry to develop products that provide maximum user control. For example, all users should be able to adjust the products to account for the varying maturity level of minors, and to adjust the list of blocked sites to reflect their own values.

It should go without saying that under no set of circumstances can governments constitutionally require anyone – whether individual users or Internet Service Providers – to run user-based blocking programs when accessing or providing access to the Internet.

Why Blocking Software Should Not Be Used by Public Libraries

The "never-ending, worldwide conversation" of the Internet, as one lower court judge called it, is a conversation in which all citizens should be entitled to participate – whether they access the Internet from the library or from the home. Just as government cannot require home users or Internet Service Providers (ISPs) to use blocking programs or self-rating programs, libraries should not require patrons to use blocking software when accessing the Internet at the library. The ACLU, like the American Library Association (ALA), opposes use of blocking software in public libraries.

Libraries have traditionally promoted free speech values by providing free books and information resources to people regardless of their age or income. Today, more than 20 percent of libraries in the United States are offering free access to the Internet, and that number is growing daily. Libraries are critical to realizing the dream of universal access to the Internet, a dream that would be drastically altered if they were forced to become Internet censors.

In a recent announcement stating its policy, the ALA said:

> Libraries are places of inclusion rather than exclusion. Current blocking/filtering software prevents not only access to what some may consider "objectionable" material, but also blocks information protected by the First Amendment. The result is that legal and useful material will inevitably be blocked.

Librarians have never been in the business of determining what their patrons should read or see, and the fact that the material is now found on Internet is no different. By installing inaccurate and unreliable blocking programs on library Internet terminals, public libraries – which are almost always governmental entities – would inevitably censor speech that patrons are constitutionally entitled to access.

It has been suggested that a library's decision to install blocking software is like other legitimate selection decisions that libraries routinely make when they add particular books to their collections. But in fact, blocking programs take selection decisions totally out of the hands of the librarian and place them in the hands of a company with no experience in library science. As the ALA noted, "(F)ilters can impose the producer's viewpoint on the community."

Because, as noted above, most filtering programs don't provide a list of the sites they block, libraries won't even know what resources are blocked. In addition, Internet speakers won't know which libraries have blocked access to their speech and won't be able to protest.

Installing blocking software in libraries to prevent adults as well as minors from accessing legally protected material raises severe First Amendment questions. Indeed, that principle – that governments can't block adult access to speech in the name of protecting children – was one of the key reasons for the Supreme Court's decision in *Reno v. ACLU.*

If adults are allowed full access, but minors are forced to use blocking programs, constitutional problems remain. Minors, especially older minors, have a constitutional right to access many of the resources that have been shown to be blocked by user-based blocking programs.

One of the virtues of the Internet is that it allows an isolated gay teenager in Des Moines, Iowa to talk to other teenagers around the globe who are also struggling with issues relating to their sexuality. It allows teens to find out how to avoid AIDS and other sexually transmitted diseases even if they are too embarrassed to ask an adult in person or even too embarrassed to check out a book.

When the ACLU made this argument in *Reno v. ACLU*, it was considered controversial, even among our allies. But the Supreme Court agreed that minors have rights too. Library blocking proposals that allow minors full access to the Internet only with parental permission are unacceptable.

Libraries can and should take other actions that are more protective of online free speech principles. First, libraries can publicize and provide links to particular sites that have been recommended for children. Second, to avoid unwanted viewing by passersby (and to protect the confidentiality of users), libraries can install Internet access terminals in ways that minimize public view. Third, libraries can impose "content-neutral" time limits on Internet use.

Conclusion

The ACLU has always favored providing Internet users, especially parents, with more information. We welcomed, for example, the American Library Association's announcement at the White House summit of The Librarian's Guide to Cyberspace for Parents and Kids, a "comprehensive brochure and Web site combining Internet terminology, safety tips, site selection advice and more than 50 of the most educational and entertaining sites available for children on the Internet."

In *Reno v. ACLU*, we noted that Federal and state governments are already vigorously enforcing existing obscenity, child pornography, and child solicitation laws on the Internet. In addition, Internet users must affirmatively seek out speech on the Internet; no one is caught by surprise.

In fact, many speakers on the Net provide preliminary information about the nature of their speech. The ACLU's site on America Online, for example, has a message on its home page announcing that the site is a "free speech zone." Many sites offering commercial transactions on the Net contain warnings concerning the security of Net information. Sites containing sexually explicit material often begin with a statement describing the adult nature of the material. Chat rooms and newsgroups have names that describe the subject being discussed. Even individual e-mail messages contain a subject line.

The preliminary information available on the Internet has several important components that distinguish it from all the ratings systems discussed above: (1) it is created and provided by the speaker; (2) it helps the user decide whether to read any further; (3) speakers who choose not to provide such information are not penalized; (4) it does not result in the automatic blocking of speech by an entity other than the speaker or reader before the speech has ever been viewed. Thus, the very nature of the Internet reveals why more speech is always a better solution than censorship for dealing with speech that someone may find objectionable.

It is not too late for the Internet community to slowly and carefully examine these proposals and to reject those that will transform the Internet from a true marketplace of ideas into just another mainstream, lifeless medium with content no more exciting or diverse than that of television.

Civil libertarians, human rights organizations, librarians and Internet users, speakers and providers all joined together to defeat the CDA. We achieved a stunning victory, establishing a legal framework that affords the Internet the highest constitutional protection. We put a quick end to a fire that was all but visible and threatening. The fire next time may be more difficult to detect – and extinguish.

Appendix: Internet Ratings Systems – How Do They Work?

The Technology: PICS, Browsers, Search Engines, and Ratings

The rating and blocking proposals discussed below all rely on a few key components of current Internet technology. While none of this technology will by itself censors speech, some of it may well enable censorship to occur.

PICS: The Platform for Internet Content Selection (PICS) is a rating standard that establishes a consistent way to rate and block online content. PICS was created by a large consortium of Internet industry leaders, and became operational last year. In theory, PICS does not incorporate or endorse any particular rating system – the technology is an empty vessel into which different rating systems can be poured. In reality, only three Third-party rating systems have been developed for PICS SafeSurf, Net Shepherd, and the de facto industry standard RSACi.

Browsers: Browsers are the software tool that Internet users need in order to access information on the World Wide Web. Two products, Microsoft's Internet Explorer and Netscape, currently control 90% of the browser market. Microsoft's Internet Explorer is now compatible with PICS. That is, the Internet Explorer can now be configured to block speech that has been rated with PICS-compatible ratings. Netscape has announced that it will soon offer the same capability. When the blocking feature on the browser is activated, speech with negative ratings is blocked. In addition, because a vast majority of Internet sites remain unrated, the blocking feature can be configured to block all unrated sites.

Search Engines: Search engines are software programs that allow Internet users to conduct searches for content on a particular subject, using a string of words or phrases. The search result typically provides a list of links to sites on the relevant topic. Four of the major search engines have announced a plan to cooperate in the move towards Internet ratings. For example, they may decide not to list sites that have negative ratings or that are unrated.

Ratings Systems: There are a few PICS-compatible ratings systems already in use. Two self-rating systems include RSACi and Safe Surf. RSACi, developed by the same group that rates video games, attempts to rate certain kinds of speech, like sex and violence, according to objective criteria describing the content. For example, it rates levels of violence from "harmless conflict; some damage to objects" to "creatures injured or killed." Levels of sexual content are rated from "passionate kissing" to "clothed sexual touching" to "explicit sexual activity; sex crimes." The context in which the material is presented is not considered under the RSACi system; for example, it doesn't distinguish educational materials from other materials.

Safe Surf applies a complicated ratings system on a variety of types of speech, from profanity to gambling. The ratings are more contextual, but they are also more subjective and value-laden. For example, Safe Surf rates sexual content from "artistic" to "erotic" to "explicit and crude pornographic."

Net Shepherd, a third-party rating system that has rated 300,000 sites, rates only for "maturity" and "quality."

Credits

The principal authors of this white paper are Ann Beeson and Chris Hansen of the ACLU Legal Department and ACLU Associate Director Barry Steinhardt. Additional editorial contributions were provided by Marjorie Heins of the Legal Department, and Emily Whitfield of the Public Education Department. This report was prepared by the ACLU Public Education Department: Loren Siegel, Director; Rozella Floranz Kennedy, Editorial Manager; Ronald Cianfaglione, Designer.

Will PICS Torch Free Speech on the Internet?

Irene Graham, Electronic Frontiers Australia

Rating and labelling of Internet content has been widely hailed as the ideal means of empowering parents to control their children's access to Internet content, without restricting adults' freedom of speech and freedom to read. Whether this is true or not, has become one of the most hotly argued topics in the Internet censorship debate.

In mid 1995, with the black cloud of the US Communications Decency Act (CDA) hanging over the Internet, the World Wide Web Consortium (W3C) began developing an Internet content labelling and selection platform. Their stated goal was to empower people worldwide to control access to online content and thereby reduce the risk of global censorship of the Internet. They announced the result of their endeavours, the Platform for Internet Content Selection (PICS), in September 1995.[1]

PICS, promoted as "Internet Access Controls Without Censorship" with emphasis on a multiplicity of rating systems, voluntary self- rating by content providers and blocking software on home computers, was enthusiastically welcomed by the Internet community.

Few people paused to consider that technological tools which empower parents to control the access of their children, equally empower totalitarian and paternalistic governments to control the access of their adult populace. Few

[1] PICS created - W3C media release http://www.w3.org/PICS/950911_Announce/pics-pr.html.

people realised that PICS compatible systems could be installed on upstream network equipment, well beyond the control of end-users.

PICS was, in fact, developed to further empower any person or entity with the power to control other peoples' access to Internet content. This includes parents, schools, universities, employers, Internet service providers and governments.

Since the first two PICS-compatible rating systems became available two years ago, few community groups, commercial organisations or individuals have evidenced interest in developing rating systems. However, governments have shown great interest in PICS, particularly the Australian Government.

Governments Hijack PICS

Less than twelve months after PICS was announced, the first indications that governments would be unable to resist the beckoning of PICS facilitated censorship systems were seen.

In early June 1996, Mr. Peter Webb, then Chairman of the Australian Broadcasting Authority (ABA), stated: "An obligation to utilise PICS-type systems, and I don't wish to imply that the ABA is endorsing the PICS system to the exclusion of any other similar or superior system, might have to be enforced."[2]

A month later, the ABA released their report on the "Investigation into the Content of On-line Services."[3] The ABA recommended, among other things, the development of a single on-line classification/rating scheme compatible with the PICS standards, for use by Australian content providers and consumers. The writers remarked that: "The support which the on-line community has expressed for the PICS system indicates that it is likely that the PICS protocol or system (or a similar protocol) will be widely and readily adopted by the Australian on-line industry and on-line users."

Unreserved support for PICS systems, then, was hardly surprising. PICS was announced just five months before submissions to the ABA inquiry closed. The first PICS compatible rating and blocking systems were not launched until after

---

[2] Speech by Peter Webb, Asian Mass Communications Research and Information Centre Conference, Singapore, 1-3 June 1996.
[3] ABA Report http://www.aba.gov.au/what/online/olsfin.htm.

the closing date. For most, perhaps all, respondents to the ABA inquiry, PICS was merely a concept; examples of the tools it enables were not available for public scrutiny.

In September 1996, Demon Internet, the largest Internet Service Provider in the UK, announced they would require all their users to rate their web pages using the RSACi rating system[4] by the end of the year. Three weeks later the "R3 Safety-Net" proposal,[5] endorsed by Internet industry associations and the UK Government, was announced. Under this scheme, Internet Service Providers (ISPs) would require all their customers to label their web pages using the RSACi rating system[6] and ISPs would remove web pages hosted on their servers which were "persistently and deliberately mis-rated."

The R3 Safety Net scheme appears to have been dropped following wide opposition to mandatory labelling and criticism of the RSACi rating system. However, in October 1997 the Internet Watch Foundation (formerly the Safety Net Foundation) announced that a large group of industry and government representatives had formed to develop a worldwide rating system.[7] The group includes the Australian Broadcasting Authority and the Recreational Software Advisory Council (RSAC) in the USA.

The prospect of mandatory self-rating and labelling heralded the beginning of a shift in attitude towards PICS. Internet users began considering a wide range of associated issues. Clearly, self-rating cannot be compelled without the application of penalties, potentially criminal penalties, for failure to rate and mis-rating. The purpose of mandating rating, and the ease of rating information correctly, therefore became relevant.

Labelling Does Not Protect Children

While many people believe that material unsuitable for children must be labelled to prevent access, this is in fact false, because PICS systems work the other way around. PICS compatible blocking programs allow access to unlabelled material,

---

[4] Demon Internet UK announcement http://www.mit.edu/activities/safe/safe/www/safe/labeling/demon/demon-censor.html.
[5] R3 Safety Net Proposal http://dtiinfo1.dti.gov.uk/safety-net/r3.htm.
[6] RSACi http://www.rsac.org.
[7] Worldwide Internet Content Labelling Development, http://www.iwf.org.uk/press/archives/p011097.html.

unless the user or administrator of the blocking program has set the controls to block access to unlabelled material.

If every document originating in every country in the world which could be deemed unsuitable for children is labelled, then allowing children to access unlabelled material would be practical. However, this is not foreseeable. Not only is it unlikely that every government will mandate labelling; criminals are unlikely to comply with such laws.

Therefore, to protect children from unsuitable material, the blocking program must be set to deny access to all unlabelled material. Otherwise, children are likely to access unsuitable content. Mandating that, for example, Playboy label photos displaying nudity is therefore pointless. Properly configured blocking programs will block access to unlabelled content anyway.

In other words, the sole purpose of labelling, with regard to children's access, is to make material available to children who are using blocking programs, not to block it. Labelling information which is suitable for children, and which publishers wish to make available to those using blocking programs, clearly has greater merit.

Mandatory Labelling is a Censorship Tool

Mandatory labelling has the potential to result in censorship by stealth.

Many providers of large quantities of information, including voluntary organisations, community groups and individuals, do not have sufficient staff or time to rate all content. These publishers would be compelled to choose between publishing less information than otherwise, or rating all content at a highly restricted level, knowing that content so labelled will be invisible to many people using blocking programs.

Content providers would also be likely to use more restrictive ratings than necessary because Internet rating systems are inherently subjective. For example, the RSACi system requires content providers to guess what a "reasonable" person would think, eg. "clothing on a male or female which a reasonable person would consider to be sexually suggestive and alluring."

Of course, content providers subject to penalties for mis-rating are likely to avail themselves of web hosting services in countries which do not mandate labelling.

Similarly, those opposed to pejoratively rating their own work, using someone else's values, may also take their business off-shore.

To Rate or Not to Rate

Whether or not governments mandate labelling, widespread usage of rating and blocking systems is likely to banish a vast range of valuable information to the fringes of cyberspace.

Rating systems claimed to be objective, such as the RSACi system, make no allowance for information of artistic, literary, scientific or educational merit. These systems require that information be rated using criteria applicable to blatant pornography and gratuitous violence. For example, a photo of Michelangelo's David, pictorial instructions on conducting breast examinations and information about safe sex, must be rated using the same criteria as applicable to photos in Hustler magazine.

Rating news reports presents similar problems. As Joshua Quittner, of The Netly News, comments: "How would you 'rate' news sites, after all? News often deals with violent situations, and occasionally with sexual themes and even adult language. How do you rate that? Do you rate every story? On deadline? Or just rate your entire site as off-limits, since sometimes you'll be covering treacherous terrain?" [8]

This conundrum led a group of news organisations in the USA, the Internet Content Coalition, to consider an "N" rating for use by "bona fide" news sites. News sites would rate all content with the "N" label thus enabling parents to choose whether to allow their children access to news. There was just one problem. Who would be given the power to decide who was a "bona fide" news site? Subsequently, in August 1997, representatives from about twenty-five news organisations, including the New York Times, Time Incorporated, the Wall Street Journal Interactive Edition, and the Associated Press, voted not only to drop the plan to create a news label, but went on record opposing Internet ratings for news sites. [9]

---

[8] Dis-Content Coalition, Joshua Quittner, The Netly News, 13 December 1996 http://cgi.pathfinder.com/time/digital/daily/0,2822,11612,00.html

[9] RSAC shelves news rating, Tim Clark and Courtney Macavinta, News.com, 10 Sep 97 http://www.news.com/News/Item/0,4,14139,00.html X-Rated Ratings?, J.D. Lasica, American Journalism Review, October 1997 http://www.newslink.org/ajrjdl21.html.

While flat refusal to self-rate may be viable for well-known sites, it may not be practical for those whose sites are generally found by using search engines.

Industry Self-regulation Causes Alarm

Shortly after the US Supreme Court struck down the CDA in June 1997, the US President convened a White House summit on Internet censorship to encourage "self-regulation" of the Internet.

At this meeting, four of the major search engines announced a plan to exclude unrated sites from search results. The president of Lycos was reported to have "thrown down the gauntlet" to the other three. Safesurf, marketers of a PICS compatible blocking program and creators of a PICS rating system, proposed an "Online Cooperative Publishing Act." Under this Act, any parent who felt their child was harmed by "negligent" publishing could sue publishers who fail to rate or mis-rate material. Parents would not be required to prove actual harm, only that the material could reasonably be required to have had a warning label or a more restrictive label.

Civil liberties organisations in several countries including the USA, UK and France have subsequently issued reports cautioning against ill-considered enthusiasm for PICS facilitated systems. In a paper titled "Fahrenheit 451.2: Is Cyberspace Burning?," the American Civil Liberties Union (ACLU) stated that they and other civil liberties organisations were "genuinely alarmed by the tenor of the White House summit and the unabashed enthusiasm for technological fixes that will make it easier to block or render invisible controversial speech." The ACLU warned:

> What may be the result? The Internet will become bland and homogenized. The major commercial sites will still be readily available they will have the resources and inclination to self-rate, and third-party rating services will be inclined to give them acceptable ratings. People who disseminate quirky and idiosyncratic speech, create individual home pages, or post to controversial news groups, will be among the first Internet users blocked by filters and made invisible by the search engines. Controversial speech will still exist, but will only be visible to

those with the tools and know-how to penetrate the dense smokescreen of industry "self-regulation."[10]

Undaunted by growing opposition to PICS, in November 1997 the W3C proposed an addition to the PICS standards called PICSRules.[11] PICSRules is a language for writing filtering rules that allow or block access to web sites. The developers envisage that individuals and organisations will develop filtering preference profiles. Internet users will then be able to select pre-configured PICS settings and install them with one click of the mouse button. In addition, PICSRules will help search engines tailor their output. Links to sites which do not meet profile criteria will be invisible to users of the profile. However, given the complexity of the PICSRules language and the few rating systems developed by individuals and organisations, it seems more likely that preference profiles will be developed by governments and installed on upstream computing equipment well beyond the control of Internet users.

During the month in which the PICSRules specification was open for public comment, members of the Global Internet Liberty Campaign (GILC) asked W3C to reject the proposals of the PICSRules Working Group, stating: "we oppose the proposed adoption of PICSRules 1.1 on the grounds that they will provide a tool for widespread global censorship, which will conflict with W3C's mission to 'realize the full potential of the Web . . . as an efficient human-human communications medium.'"[12]

Despite the concerns raised, the W3C approved PICSRules.

W3C representatives defend PICS and PICSRules on the ground that they are merely technical standards. They express the view that it is the role of others to ensure that PICS technologies are not used to control societies. PICS critics contend that PICS is more than a mere technical standard; it is a standard developed with the express purpose of making the architecture of the Internet censor friendly. As such, PICS technologies raise fundamental issues about free speech which should be debated in public. W3C, an organisation of industry and government representatives, readily acknowledge that they have not adopted the

[10] Fahrenheit 451.2: Is Cyberspace Burning? How Rating and Blocking Proposals, May Torch Free Speech on the Internet, ACLU, August 1997 http://www.aclu.org/issues/cyber/burning.html.
[11] PICSRules Media Release, November 1997 http://www.w3.org/Press/Internet_Summit.
[12] GILC submission on PICSRules, December 1997
http://www.gilc.org/speech/ratings/gilc-pics-submission.html.

position that unrestricted access to information is a fundamental human right that transcends national sovereignty.

For many years, the Net community has proclaimed that the Net treats censorship as damage and routes around it. Until a means of routing around PICS becomes widely available, people concerned about threats to free speech would be well advised to shine the hot light of public scrutiny on W3C and governments interested in PICS. PICS, like the now dead CDA that kindled it, threatens to torch a large segment of the Internet community.

Sites Censored by Censorship Software

Peacefire

A partial collection of web sites that have been added to the "bad site" lists of one or more blocking products.

The National Organization for Women -- the best-known example of a site blocked by a blocking program for its political content. CYBERsitter CEO Brian Milburn said in a C-Net article that the N.O.W. site was blocked for maintaining information about gay and lesbian rights.

The Electronic Frontier Foundation -- the organization behind the online blue ribbon campaign for free speech on the Internet. Cyber Patrol blocked their site for several months for reasons that the software company has never disclosed. Ironically, the Cyber Patrol web site displays the EFF blue ribbon, superimposed over the Cyber Patrol logo.

Mother Jones magazine, the online version of a widely read progressive magazine which was blocked by CYBERsitter for running a story on gay rights. CYBERsitter later unblocked their site. motherjones.com was also briefly put on Cyber Patrol's CyberNOT list and then removed.

Nizkor is an online memorial to victims of the Holocaust; the site's name is a Hebrew word for "we will remember." Their site was blocked for a number of months by Cyber Patrol before the block was removed without any explanation.

Peacefire was blocked by CYBERsitter in December 1996 for hosting the page "CYBERsitter: Where Do We Not Want You To Go Today?" The subsequent controversy was the subject of an article in Wired News on December 10, 1996.

The Ethical Spectacle was blocked by CYBERsitter for hosting a mirror of our CYBERsitter page at http://www.spectacle.org/alert/peace.html.

The International Gay and Lesbian Human Rights Commission was blocked by CYBERsitter for gay rights advocacy.

The MIT Student Association for Freedom of Expression was blocked by Cyber Patrol for several months. SAFE maintains pages that are critical of Cyber Patrol and other filtering schemes.

The HIV/AIDS Information Center of the Journal of the American Medical Association is blocked by Cyber Patrol.

The Penal Lexicon, a British site advocating prisoners' rights in the U.K., is blocked by CYBERsitter.

The National Rifle Association was given an "adult" rating from Net Shepherd. According to Net Shepherd's database, the site is now "unrated."

HotWired, the online version of Wired magazine, was blocked for several months by Cyber Patrol.

The Gay and Lesbian Alliance Against Defamation (GLAAD) was added to CYBERsitter's list of blocked sites in April 1997. The GLAAD site was also given an "adult" rating from Net Shepherd, which was later retracted.

Planned Parenthood is blocked by Cyber Patrol, despite the fact that they are plaintiffs in the same joint lawsuit against the Communications Decency Act.

Envirolink, an online environmental activism network, was blocked by Cyber Patrol for the images and text in the Animal Rights Resource Site, describing violations of animal rights in laboratory testing.

The Human Rights Campaign, a campaign for gay/lesbian rights in the United States, was given an "adult" rating from Net Shepherd, later retracted.

Word filtering: CYBERsitter filters "offensive language" -- obviously includes the Seven Dirty Words but also the phrases "gay rights," "safe sex," "homosexual," "lesbian," and "fairy." After adding Peacefire to their "bad site" list, CYBERsitter also began blocking the words "Peacefire," "Bennett Haselton" and "Don't buy CYBERsitter." Cyber Patrol, slightly less restrictive, blocks URLs that contain the word "sex" -- which includes all Yahoo! page listings about equal rights for "lesbians, gays and bisexuals."

Who Watches the Watchmen: Internet Content Rating Systems, and Privatised Censorship

Cyber-Rights & Cyber-Liberties (UK)

Introduction

After much recent publicity concerning the availability of materials on the Internet that are offensive to many people (racist and Nazi propaganda, pornography, and information on disrupting train travel), Internet content rating systems are developing with broad support by the government agencies and by the industry but without much public debate over their utility or about their long-term implications. Civil liberties proponents in many countries who have examined content-control proposals have found them to be much more intrusive and restrictive than the supporters of rating systems and filtering software claim. The proposed systems often exceed their makers' claims in the types of content restricted, the number and type of people prevented from reaching content, the technical changes required to public electronic networks, and the burdens on providers of content or Internet service providers.

Recently the UK Internet Watch Foundation ("IWF") convened an advisory board comprising representatives of content providers, children's charities, regulators from other media, Internet Service Providers and civil liberties groups, to propose a UK-focused system for rating Internet content. (See House of Commons, 26 June 1997, Written Answers, Internet).

Cyber-Rights & Cyber-Liberties (UK), a non-profit civil liberties organisation which promotes free speech and privacy related issues on the Internet, has recently discovered that no "civil liberties" organisations are in fact involved in the development of rating systems at the UK level. It has been wrongly stated many times by the media, by members of the Parliament, and in different EU reports. that UK civil liberties organisations are involved with the development of rating systems and that they have been also consulted on these issues.

It is the purpose of this report to explain why the debates on regulation of Internet content should take place openly and with the involvement of the public at large rather than at the hands of a few industry based private bodies.

A Short History of Content Regulation and Content Blocking Technology

Until the 1990s there were no restrictions on Internet content. Governments did not concern themselves because Internet access was available mainly to a relatively small (though international) community of academics and engineers at universities, government research institutions, and commercial research institutions.

Despite the largely serious and academic nature of most material, a sub-culture also flourished of odd sexually-oriented, politically-oriented, and other materials often considered "wacko" (insane). The presence of such materials was tolerated by all users and even considered a sign of the health of the medium. In particular, few people were bothered by the presence of pornography in a community made up over 90% of male users.

When the Internet became more widespread and governments began to take notice, the first stage in Internet content control began, consisting of heavy-handed and repressive forays in censorship. The US Communications Decency Act 1996 was a part of this trend, as are more recent but similar proposals by the Australian government.

The first wave of direct censorship ran its course, turned back by concerns over its effects on free expression (the CDA was declared to infringe on constitutionally protected speech, see *Reno v. ACLU*, 117 S. Ct. 2329 (1997)) as well as its technological inappropriateness for the medium and its ineffectiveness in a global environment.

The second stage in content control thus began with the introduction of rating and filtering products that claim to permit users to block unwanted material from their personal systems. The most sophisticated and widely recognised of these systems is the Platform for Internet Content Selection ("PICS"), introduced by the World Wide Web Consortium. European governments were especially interested in this hoped-for solution. They backed away quickly from incidents in the first stage of direct suppression and put forward PICS and rating systems as a proposed standard, both through national governments and the European Union as a self-regulatory solution to Internet content.

There are many problems, however, in rating and filtering systems as will be explained in this report. They are crude and tend to block too many sites. Most focus on the World Wide Web, offering no way to block objectionable content on other distribution mechanisms of the Internet such as newsgroups and ftp sites. Each system is extremely subjective and affected by cultural assumptions, so international exchanges of systems will not satisfy users. Finally, the systems were designed for individual users and do not scale well to use by entire countries and third parties.

Thus, we are beginning to see a third stage emerge in content control: that of international co-operation to remove content from the Internet. For some clearly delineated materials, such as sexually explicit material in which children are actors, such co-operation may be helpful. However, as a general trend this stage is fraught with danger. The public is not likely to support the suppression of material that is legal in their own country but illegal in another.

EURIM Report and Proposed Legislation

EURIM, a UK body made up of members of parliament, industry representatives and special interest groups, set up a working party to examine illegal content earlier this year. EURIM published a report entitled, "Internet Content Regulation," in July 1997 which found that existing regulations are inadequate to cover the new medium of the Internet.

"There is a need to clarify and refine our existing laws on illegal material. The application of such laws to the Net . . . is not particularly clear . . . but even when the law is clear, we must ensure that those whose job it is to uphold it, our police forces, are given the equipment and specialist training they need," said Baroness Dean, EURIM council representative.

The EURIM Report recommends the strengthening of the Internet Watch Foundation (IWF), or the setting up of a statutory body to monitor the Internet industry. The report states that "the IWF is not independent from the ISPs and lacks the credibility and influence which formal recognition and legal status could give." Tory MP Ian Bruce, vice-chairman of EURIM and a member of the

Parliamentary IT Committee, said he aimed for the watchdog to have "legislative teeth" – to cope with cases where Internet service providers refuse to act voluntarily against an offending source. Bruce also suggested it might be necessary to set up an "OFNET", along the lines of OFTEL, to take over the IWF's regulatory work. (See Computing, "MPs act to curb Net abuse," 10 September 1997).

Cyber-Rights & Cyber-Liberties (UK) does not agree that the existing laws need to be clarified to cover the new medium. UK defamation laws were recently updated with the new Defamation Act 1996 and it clarifies the liability of ISPs. The Sexual Offences (Conspiracy & Incitement) Act 1996 refers to the use of the Internet and the child pornography laws is more than adequate to deal with the availability and dissemination of this kind of material on the Internet. There have been many prosecutions following "Operation Starburst" in the UK.

I. No Pressing Need in Fact

A new bill was presented in the UK Parliament by Mrs. Ann Winterton on Internet (Dissemination of Child Pornography) in June 1997 and this would create new rules that are more restrictive and oppressive on the Internet than in other media. Restrictive legislation of this kind should be resisted as fears and impressions of illegal trafficking on the Internet are exaggerated. Between December 1996 and June 1997, about 1000 illegal items were reported to the Internet Watch Foundation, but only 9 reports involving 75 of them originated from the UK. Therefore, there is no need for heavy-handed legislation involving the dissemination of child pornography on the Internet as most of the illegal content available on the Internet does not originate from the UK. There is also no need for expensive monitoring of the Internet at a national level as the few problems created by the Internet remain global ones.

A recent European Commission working paper agreed and stated that "there is no legal vacuum as regards the protection of minors and human dignity, not even in online and Internet services. According to the principle of territorial jurisdiction, the law applies on the national territory of the State and hence also applies to online services." (see Commission Staff Working paper, "Protection of Minors and Human Dignity in Audio-visual and Information Services: Consultation on the Green Paper," SEC (97) 1203, Brussels, June 1997).

II. National Legislation is the Wrong Response

However, we do recognise that the Internet is a global medium which does not respect boundaries, and that individual nation-states are losing their capacity for governance. Therefore, heavy handed new legislation at a national level will in any event be inadequate and ineffective. All nations have an important part to play in the fight against internationally defined illegal material, such as forms of child pornography. Although the UK police have been successful with "Operation Starburst" in identifying an international paedophile ring, substantial collaboration at an international level may be needed to fight child pornography between various national police forces. This can be achieved, as suggested by the European Commission, initially at the EU level. Therefore, it is not in the best interest of the UK Parliament to legislate on these matters just because there is a public outcry and moral panic.

III. Confusion between Illegal and Harmful Content

The regulation of potentially "harmful content" such as pornography on the Internet and regulation of invariably illegal content such as child pornography are different in nature and should not be confused. Child pornography is banned in a wide range of countries because its creation involves child abuse. Other types of offensive content, by contrast, are "victimless crimes" and have no proven ill-effects on other people. For example, a link between the consumption of pornography and sexual abuse has never been established (see e.g. Dennis Howitt and Guy Cumberbatch, Pornography: Impacts and Influences, Research and Planning Unit London: HMSO, 1990). This distinction explains why there is a wide variation among countries (and local communities within those countries) about what is tolerable in pornography involving adults.

IV. Adults Should not be Treated Like Children

Any regulatory action intended to protect a certain group of people, such as children, should not take the form of an unconditional prohibition of using the Internet to distribute content that is freely available to adults in other media. Therefore, attempts to pass online censorship legislation such as the US Communications Decency Act (part of the 1996 Telecommunications Act) should be avoided and child pornography laws should not be used as false examples of supposed legitimate restriction of freedom of expression. The US Supreme Court recently stated in *Reno v. ACLU*, 117 S. Ct. 2329 (1997) that the Internet is not as "invasive" as radio or television and confirmed the finding of the lower court that "communications over the Internet do not 'invade' an individual"s home or appear on one's computer screen unbidden. Users seldom encounter content by accident." Partly on the basis of this user-driven aspect of the Internet, the court unanimously struck down the Communications Decency Act, which tried to restrict the distribution of "indecent" material.

This report will now proceed to examine the technical means of restricting content which have been widely proposed as a self-regulatory solution instead of "top-down" regulatory restrictions.

Self-regulatory Solutions for the Internet

There appears not to be a single solution for the regulation of illegal and harmful content on the Internet because, for example, the exact definition of offences such as child pornography varies from one country to another.

These are pressing issues of public, political, commercial and legal interest. The treatment of material considered harmful may be different in different societies, and what is considered to be harmful depends on cultural differences. It is therefore imperative that international initiatives take into account different ethical standards in different countries in order to explore appropriate rules to protect people against offensive material. For example, the European Court of Human Rights in Handyside (see Handyside case (1976) 19 Y.B.E.C. 506) stated that the steps necessary in a democratic society for the protection of morals will depend on the type of morality to which a country is committed. A Recent European Commission Communication Paper (1996) stated that "each country may reach its own conclusion in defining the borderline between what is permissible and not permissible". A conflict always exists between the desire to allow free expression and the feeling that morality must be enforced. Each society must decide where to draw the line. However, a good rule of thumb is that free expression is more important to a healthy and free society, and should not be seriously harmed by attempts to enforce to moral standards.

In this context it might be useful to quote from one of the more recent judgements of the European Court of Human Rights in *Castells v. Spain* (judgement of 23 April 1992, Series A no. 236, p.22, § 42):

> . . . freedom of expression constitutes one of the essential
> foundations of a democratic society, one of the basic conditions
> for its progress. Subject to paragraph 2 of Article 10 [of the
> European Convention on Human Rights], it is applicable not

only to "information" or "ideas" that are favourably received or regarded as inoffensive or as a matter of indifference but also to those that offend, shock or disturb. Such are the demands of that pluralism, tolerance or broadmindedness without which there is no democratic society.

"Harm" is a criterion which will depend upon cultural differences. There have been attempts, for example, by the German government to restrict the availability of hate speech on the Internet, specifically the web sites related to the denial of the Holocaust. Many of these same materials are legal in other countries, even though most of the population finds them offensive. The preservation of the principle of free expression should be more important than the pursuit and prosecution of every potentially dangerous speaker.

Self-regulation is an appropriate tool to address the criteria of harmful content. Dealing with illegal material is a matter for the courts and the law enforcement agencies. (see House of Lords, Select Committee on Science and Technology "Information Society: Agenda for Action in the UK," Session 1995-96, 5th Report, London: HMSO, 23 July 1996, para 4.163).

"Self-regulation in this field has a number of advantages. Rules devised by the media are more likely to be internalised and accepted. In addition, it may avoid heavy-handed legal intervention which carries with it the spectre of government censorship." (See Walker, Clive "Fundamental Rights, Fair Trials and the New Audio-Visual Sector" [1996] MLR 59, 4, 517-539.)

A self-regulatory model for harmful content on the Internet may include the following levels and in this model "self" means as in "individual" without the state involvement:

- User or Parental Responsibility

- Parental Software

On the other hand we offer the following models for fighting such illegal content as forms of child pornography on the Internet and this is a more collective solution different from the above model:

- User Responsibility to report it

- Hotlines for reporting

- Code of Conduct by ISPs

- National Legislation - distribution

- International Level - Co-operation

There is no need for rating systems to be used for illegal content and the next sections explain why there is no need for rating systems to be used for harmful content on the Internet.

Rating Systems

There have been recent calls in Europe for the regulation of the Internet and these are relevant to the UK developments. Recently European Commission approved a Communication on Illegal and Harmful Content on the Internet (1996) and a Green Paper (1996) on the protection of minors and human dignity in the context of new electronic services in October 1996. The European Commission documents follow the resolution adopted by the Telecommunications Council of Ministers in September 1996, on preventing the dissemination of illegal content on the Internet, especially child pornography. While the Communication gives policy options for immediate action to fight against harmful and illegal content on the Internet, the Green Paper sets out to examine the challenges that society faces in ensuring that these issues of overriding public interest are adequately taken into account in the rapidly evolving world of audiovisual and information services.

The European Commission Communication Paper suggested that:

> the answer to the challenge will be a combination of self-control of the service providers, new technical solutions such as rating systems and filtering software, awareness actions for parents and teachers, information on risks and possibilities to limit these risks and of international co-operation.

All these initiatives at the European level were adopted in a Resolution at the Telecommunications Council of November 1996. The European Parliament also adopted a resolution following these initiatives. The UK Government welcomed the Communication with its emphasis on self-regulation by industry, as entirely consistent with the UK"s approach:

The UK strongly agrees with the Commission that since a legal framework for regulation of the Internet already exists in Member States, new laws or regulations are unnecessary. (Select Committee on European Legislation, 1996, para 14.8)

Cyber-Rights & Cyber-Liberties (UK) argues that a radical self-regulatory solution for the hybrid Internet content should not include any kind of rating systems and self-regulatory solutions should include minimum government and industry involvement.

Platform for Internet Content Selections ("PICS") is a rating system for the Internet and is similar to the V-chip technology for filtering out violence or pornography on television systems. PICS is widely supported by various governments and industry based organisations such as the Internet Watch Foundation in the UK. PICS works by embedding electronic labels in the text or image documents to vet their content before the computer displays them or passes them on to another computer. The vetting system could include political, religious, advertising or commercial topics. These can be added by the publisher of the material, by the company providing access to the Internet, or by an independent vetting body.

Currently (as of November 1997), there are three PICS related rating systems that are being widely used or promoted:

> **RSACi**: The most common scheme for screening material was developed by the United States based Recreational Software Advisory Council on the Internet ("RSACi"), originally a scheme for rating computer games. It rates material according to the degree of sex, violence, nudity, and bad language depicted. It is usually this PICS/RSACi screening combination that people have in mind when they refer to PICS. As of September 1997, RSACi claims to have over 43,000 sites rated.

> **SafeSurf**: Developed by the SafeSurf corporation, this system's categories include "Age Range", "Profanity", "Heterosexual Themes", "Homosexual Themes", "Nudity", "Violence," "Sex, Violence, and Profanity", "Intolerance", "Glorifying Drug Use", "Other Adult Themes", and "Gambling", with 9 distinctions for each category.

SafeSurf and RSACi both rely on self-rating of Internet sites by web publishers. While apparently being voluntary and fair, this kind of system is likely to end up being a serious burden on content providers. First, the only way to deal with incorrect ratings is to prosecute content providers. That is very dangerous and an infringement on free speech. Secondly, ISPs and search engines will simply block any unrated sites, so that content providers will feel it necessary to rate their sites even if they oppose the system.

> **NetShepherd**: Based in Calgary, Net Shepherd rates sites based on maturity levels (General, Child, Pre-teen, Teen, Adult, and Objectionable), and quality levels (1-5 stars). Unlike SafeSurf and RSAC, NetShepherd conducts third-party ratings of web sites. NetShepherd claim to have rated over 300,000 sites. NetShepherd has also announced partnerships with firms such as Altavista and Catholic Telecom, Inc.

The EURIM Report encourages the development of internationally accepted rating systems so that some sort of "harmful content" may be controlled at the point of access. The Internet Watch Foundation ("IWF"), was seen as a possible way forward on this subject by the EURIM report and the IWF has been working on the introduction of these rating systems together with its European partners (including ECO, the German Electronic Commerce Forum and Childnet International, the UK-based charity) under the Internet Content Rating for Europe ("INCORE") project.

This initiative aims to: (1) create a forum of interested groups to investigate content rating (identifying illegal and classifying legal material. A key element of this will be consumer research as to users' expectations regarding the Internet and, more specifically, the kind of material they would consider to be appropriate to apply ratings to); (2) draw together self-regulatory bodies as hot-line organisations; and (3) consider European input into world-wide standards.

Child pornography is often used as an excuse to regulate the Internet but there is no need to rate illegal content such as child pornography since it is forbidden for any conceivable audience and this kind of illegal content should be regulated by the enforcement of existing UK laws. On the other hand, the Internet contains other kind of content which would be legal but otherwise defined as harmful for instance to children.

According to the Internet Watch Foundation, there is "a whole category of dangerous subjects" that require ratings and these are information related to drugs, sex, violence, information about dangerous sports like bungee-jumping, and hate speech material (see Wired News, "Europe Readies Net Content Ratings," 7 July, 1997). It is surprising to see bomb-making material being omitted from this list, but we can expect it to be added to the list as happened recently in the US. Senator Dianne Feinstein, in the United States introduced legislation specifically making it illegal to distribute bomb-making information on the Internet. This legislation was found unconstitutional in the US and it should be noted that this kind of information, including the Anarchist"s Cookbook are available through well known bookshops such as Waterstones and Dillons within the UK.

We also warn that self-rating systems must not be used as a pretext for "zoning" the Internet, as two dissenting justices suggested in the U.S. Supreme Court, *Reno v. ACLU*, 1 17 S. Ct. 2329 (1997). The dissenting argument, while agreeing that the CDA was unconstitutional, left open the possibility that material could in the future be banned from the open Internet and allowed only in special sites where access would be controlled by identification and screening of users. This proposal is onerous for several reasons: it threatens to restrict socially valuable information that the government does not wish people to see, and requires users to reveal their identities when viewing sensitive materials such as information on sexually transmitted diseases or information for victims of AIDS. This kind of violation would have serious implications for privacy of online users and also would have a chilling effect on use of the Internet.

Recently in the USA, the American Civil Liberties Union was alarmed because of the failure to examine the longer term implications for the Internet of rating and blocking schemes. The ACLU published a white paper in August 1997 entitled "Fahrenheit 451.2: Is Cyberspace Burning? How Rating and Blocking Proposals May Torch Free Speech on the Internet" (contained in this volume). The ACLU paper warned that government-coerced, industry efforts to rate content on the Internet could torch free speech online.

"In the physical world, people censor the printed word by burning books," said Barry Steinhardt, Associate Director of the ACLU and one of the paper's authors. "But in the virtual world, you can just as easily censor controversial speech by banishing it to the farthest corners of cyberspace with blocking and rating schemes." According to the ACLU, third-party ratings systems pose free speech problems and with few third-party rating products currently available, the potential for arbitrary censorship increases. The white paper was distributed with an open letter from Steinhardt to members of the Internet community. "It is not too late for the Internet community to slowly and carefully examine these proposals and to reject those that will transform the Internet from a true marketplace of ideas into just another mainstream, lifeless medium."

The ACLU white paper gave six reasons why self-rating schemes are wrong for the Internet and Cyber-Rights & Cyber-Liberties (UK) endorses these statements:

1) Self-rating schemes will cause controversial speech to be censored.

2) Self-rating is burdensome, unwieldy, and costly.

3) Conversation cannot be rated.

4) Self-rating will create "Fortress America" on the Internet.

5) Self-ratings will only encourage, not prevent, government regulation.

6) Self-ratings schemes will turn the Internet into a homogenised medium dominated by commercial speakers.

It seems likely that there will be many rating authorities, and different communities will consider the same web pages to be in different PICS/RSACi categories. Some rating authorities may judge a certain site as an offensive even though it has a socially valuable purpose, such as web sites dealing with sexual abuse and AIDS. This would mean that there will be no space for free speech arguments and dissent because the ratings will be done by private bodies and the government will not be involved "directly."

The governments do not need to either impose rating systems and rating bodies with different cultural backgrounds, nor get involved in their development.

Parents Should be Responsible for Protecting Children

The prime responsibility for assuring an appropriate moral environment for children must rest elsewhere. Parents and teachers should be responsible for protecting children from accessing pornographic content which may be harmful to their development. Standards that are overly broad or loose will result if the job is handed over to rating bodies with different cultural backgrounds, the software industry, or even the producers of pornography. This is not a helpless demand for personal responsibility, since the computer industry is also supplying the means of protection.

Most filtering software available is designed for the home market. These are intended to respond to the preferences of parents making decisions for their own children. There are currently 15 blocking and filtering products and these are mainly US based (see http://www.netparents.org/software/) and do not represent the cultural differences in a global environment such as the Internet.

It has been reported many times that, this kind of software is over-inclusive and limits access to or censors inconvenient web sites, or filters potentially educational materials regarding AIDS and drug abuse prevention. Therefore, "censorware" enters homes despite the hype over "parental control" as an alternative to government censorship. The companies creating this kind of software also provide no appeal system to content providers who are "banned," thereby "subverting the self-regulating exchange of information that has been a hallmark of the Internet community." (see CPSR letter dated 18 December 1996 sent to Solid Oak, the makers of CyberSitter at http://www.cpsr.org/cpsr/nii/cyber-rights/)

Therefore, such software should not be used in public and university libraries because libraries are responsible for serving a broad and diverse community with different preferences and views. American Library Association in a resolution adopted in June 1997, stated that "blocking Internet sites is antithetical to library missions because it requires the library to limit information access."

We recommend that any filtering system should be market driven by the local industries, without government interference and that the local industries creating these kind of parental tools should be open and accountable to the online users.

The Role of Self-Regulatory Bodies such as the Internet Watch Foundation

Internet Watch Foundation, supported by the UK Government, was announced in September 1996 and it follows up a similar initiative in Holland (see below) although there are differences between the two hotline systems. While the Dutch hotline is established by the Dutch Foundation for Internet Providers ("NLIP"), Dutch Internet users, the National Criminal Intelligence Service ("CRI"), National Bureau against Racial Discrimination and a psychologist, the UK Internet Watch Foundation ("IWF") is predominantly industry based.

The Dutch Model

The Dutch hotline has been operating quite successfully since June 1996, resulting in a substantial reduction of the amount of child pornography pictures distributed from Holland and resulting in the actual prosecution of authors, in close co-operation with the police. Furthermore, a procedure has been developed to deal with child pornography originating from other countries than the Netherlands. In case such complaint is sent to the hot-line, the foreign author and service provider are notified. If this action does not lead to the actual removal of the content, the Dutch police, after being informed by a representative of the hot-line, notifies their colleagues in the country of origination.

The Metropolitan Police in London has a free confidential telephone hot-line (0800-789321) to combat terrorism, and a similar step should have been taken to combat child pornography and child sexual abuse whether related to the Internet or not. This would have had a general purpose. The idea of removing materials containing child pornography from the Internet at UK level seems not to be a solution in a multi-national environment. The IWF is playing with fire as their possible future involvement with other kinds of content which may be offensive but totally legal, may set up a dangerous unprecedented act of privatised censorship where there is no space for dissent.

IWF has an e-mail, telephone and fax hot-line for users to be able to report materials related to child pornography and other obscene materials. IWF, informs all British ISPs once they locate the "undesirable content." The ISPs will have no excuse in law of being unaware of the offending material and the UK police will probably take action against those ISPs who do not remove the relevant content requested from IWF.

In contrast to the Dutch Model, the IWF proposals state that the UK ISPs should bear responsibility for their services and they need to implement reasonable, practicable and proportionate measures to hinder the use of the Internet for illegal purposes. But it is wrong to assume that ISPs should be responsible for content provided by the third parties on the Internet.

There are also technical problems with the utility of the IWF initiatives where on-line users will report the unwanted materials. Users will probably report material unacceptable according to their taste and moral views, but it should be remembered that it is for the Courts and judges to decide whether something is obscene or illegal. It should also be noted that with reporting systems the interpretation of images will always be subjective. IWF also promotes and recommends the use of rating systems such as PICS (see above) but industry based organisations backed up by governments do not need to either impose rating systems and rating bodies with different cultural backgrounds, nor get involved in their development. The application and utility of the IWF will have to be assessed and maybe reviewed.

Internet Service Providers' Liability

ISPs differ in nature in different countries, but the main aim remains the provision of Internet related services to the online users. Technically it is not possible to access the Internet without the services of an ISP and therefore the role of the ISPs is crucial to access the Internet. The crucial role they play in providing access to the Internet made them visible targets for the control of "content regulation" on the Internet.

A recent European Commission Communication to the European Parliament, The Council, The Economic and Social Committee and the Committee of the Regions on Illegal and Harmful Content on the Internet, (1996) stated that "Internet access providers and host service providers play a key role in giving users access to Internet content. It should not however be forgotten that the prime responsibility for content lies with authors and content providers."

Blocking access at the level of access providers has been criticised by the EU communication paper on the ground that these actions go far beyond the limited category of illegal content and "such a restrictive regime is inconceivable for Europe as it would severely interfere with the freedom of the individual and its political traditions." Therefore "the law may need to be changed or clarified to assist access providers and host service providers, whose primary business is to provide a service to customers."

The EU developments are very important and would affect both the UK and other Member States. "Therefore, the position of the ISPs should be clarified, and they should not be targeted by the individual governments and law enforcement bodies where the ISPs have no control of the Internet content."

Two technical factors prevent a service provider, such as the CompuServe branch prosecuted twice in Germany over the past two years, from blocking the free flow of information on the Internet. First, an Internet service provider cannot easily stop the incoming flow of material and the thousands of unsolicited commercial e-mails that go through the systems of the ISPs is a good example of this. No one can monitor the enormous quantity of network traffic, which may consist of hundreds of thousands of emails, newsgroup messages, files, and Web pages that pass through in dozens of text and binary formats, some of them readable only by particular proprietary tools. As the European Commission noted recently, "it is as yet unclear how far it is technically possible to block access to content once it is identified as illegal. This is a problem which also affects the degree of liability of the access providers."

A second technical problem is that a provider cannot selectively disable transmission to particular users. Electronic networks typically do not allow for the identification of particular users or their national region. Thus, CompuServe correctly claimed that it cannot provide material in one country while blocking it in another; such a distinction would require an enormous new infrastructure on top of the current network.

Some networking technologies, such as newsgroups, may allow individual operators to select some groups or items and block others. But many technologies, such as the widely used World Wide Web, currently do not support such selectivity.

The recent "Bonn Declaration" underlined the importance of clearly defining the relevant legal rules on responsibility for content of the various actors in the chain between creation and use. The Declaration recognised the need to make a clear distinction between the responsibility of those who produce and place content in circulation and that of intermediaries such as the Internet Service Providers. (see <http://www2.echo.lu/bonn/ final.html>.)

The current situation at the UK does not represent a self-regulatory solution as suggested by the UK Government. It is moving towards a form of censorship, a privatised and industry based one where there will be no space for dissent as it will be done by the use of private organisations, rating systems and at the entry level by putting pressure on the UK Internet Service Providers. One can only recall the events which took place in the summer of 1996 and how the ISPs were pressured by the Metropolitan police to remove around 130 newsgroups from their servers.

Policing the Internet and the Role of the UK Police

Internet related crimes are not a priority for the UK police forces while there is an insatiable demand for the bobby on the beat and reduction of the street crimes such as car thefts are a priority. Considering the international aspect of the Internet, it would not be only up to the UK police, or any other police force in its own to try to patrol the Internet.

The action taken by the UK Metropolitan police in August 1996 to censor usenet discussion groups was ill-considered and did not reduce the availability of pornographic content on the Internet. The list of newsgroups provided by the UK police included much material that is not illegal, such as legitimate discussion groups for homosexuals, and discussion groups which do not contain any pictures, but contain text, sexual fantasies and stories. These would almost certainly not infringe UK obscenity laws. The action of the Metropolitan police also amounts to censorship of material without any public debate. Any action with regard to regulation of the Internet should take place following informed debate and policy-making by Parliament and not by the police (or the industry itself). Sensible action by the UK government is needed to resolve the problem rather than censoring or banning distasteful material on the Internet and it is wrong to treat the ISPs as "usual suspects" for the provision of illegal content on the Internet.

Conclusion

With rating systems and the moral panic behind the Internet content, the Internet could be transformed into a "family friendly" medium, just like the BBC. But it should be remembered that the Internet is not as intrusive as the TV and users seldom encounter illegal content such as child pornography. Like other historical forms of censorship, current attempts to define and ban objectionable content are vague and muddy, reaching out far beyond their reasonable targets to hurt the promise of open communication systems.

Government-imposed censorship, over-regulation, or service provider liability will do nothing to keep people from obtaining material the government does not like, as most of it will be on servers in another country (as happened recently with the availability of the JET Report in 37 different web sites on the Internet outside the UK). Such restrictions would, however, make Britain, like any other jurisdiction that goes too far, a very hostile place for network development or any other high-tech industry and investment.

If there is anyone who needs to be educated on Internet matters, it is the government officials, the police and MPs together with the media in the first place but not online users, parents and children. We do not need moral crusaders under the guise of industry based organisations to decide what is acceptable and not acceptable.

Child pornography is another matter, and its availability and distribution should be regulated whether on the Internet and elsewhere. But the main concern should remain the prevention of child abuse – the involvement of children in the making of pornography or its use to groom them to become involved in abusive acts, rather than discussion and fantasy. It was reported recently by the Home Department that the National Criminal Intelligence Service ("NCIS") Paedophile Section has spent £53,027 (1995-96) and £61,672 (1996-97) for gathering information on all forms of paedophile activity. More money should be spent to gather information about paedophiles and online paedophilia activity rather than spending the available resources on developing rating systems.

When censorship is implemented by government threat in the background, but run by private parties, legal action is nearly impossible, accountability difficult, and the system is not open and becomes undemocratic. These are sensitive issues and therefore, before introducing these systems there should be an open public debate possibly together with a consultation paper from the DTI. It should be noted that the IWF is predominantly industry based and therefore it does not necessarily represent the public at large and the UK society.

Bibliography and Further Online Resources

Akdeniz, Yaman, "The Regulation of Pornography and Child Pornography on the Internet" 1997 (1) The Journal of Information, Law and Technology (JILT). http://elj.warwick.ac.uk/jilt/internet/97_1akdz/

American Civil Liberties Union, Fahrenheit 451.2: Is Cyberspace Burning? How Rating and Blocking Proposals May Torch Free Speech on the Internet, August 1997 http://www.aclu.org/issues/cyber/burning.html

Computer Professionals for Social Responsibility Question Internet Filtering Agreement, July 18, 1997, at http://www.cpsr.org/dox/issues/filters.html

EURIM is an association of Parliamentarians and businesses established to advance the UK"s contribution to pan-European informatics (information technology and related products, services and issues) and telematics (electronic communication whether by wire, febre or wavelength and the products services and materials transmitted over thes neworks) and to act as a link between parliamentarians, commerce and industry, Whitehall and Brussels. At the start of 1995, members of EURIM included over 75 Mps, MEPs and Peers from all parties plus over 40 Corporate Members and Not-for-profit and Small Firm Associates.

EURIM web pages are at <http://www.eurim.org/>. EURIM Briefing No 19 : The Regulation of Content on the Internet, July 1997.

European Commission Communication to the European Parliament, The Council, The Economic and Social Committee and the Committee of the Regions: Illegal and Harmful Content on the Internet, Com (96) 487, Brussels, 16 October 1996.

European Commission Green Paper on the Protection of Minors and Human Dignity in Audovisual and Information Services, Brussels, 16 October 1996.

European Commission Working Party Report (1996) "Illegal and Harmful Content on the Internet"

EPIC Censorware pages at http://www.epic.org/free_speech/censorware/

Filtering Facts, a web site which supports the idea of filtering on the Internet, http://www.filteringfacts.org/index.htm

Finkelstein, Seth, "The Truth Isn't Out There," http://www.spectacle.org/cs/seth.html

Internet Watch Foundation is available at http://www.internetwatch.org.uk/

Lessig, Lawrence , Tyranny in the Infrastructure: The CDA was bad - but PICS may be worse, Wired, Issue 5.07, July 1997.

Peacefire, a US organisation which opposes blocking software, http://www.peacefire.org/info/blocking_software.shtml

Wallace, Jonathan, The Censorware Page at http://www.spectacle.org/cs/

Credits

Cyber-Rights & Cyber-Liberties (UK) Report, "Watching the Watchmen: Internet Content Rating Systems, Hotlines and Privatised Censorship" was written by Yaman Akdeniz. Professor Clive Walker, Centre for Criminal Justice Studies, University of Leeds, Ms. Louise Ellison, Faculty of Law, University of Manchester and Mr. Andrew Oram, Computer Professionals for Social Responsibility (USA) contributed to this report.

Faulty Filters: How Content Filters Block Access to Kid-Friendly Information on the Internet

Electronic Privacy Information Center

Executive Summary

In order to determine the impact of software filters on the open exchange of information on the Internet, the Electronic Privacy Information Center conducted 100 searches using a traditional search engine and then conducted the same 100 searches using a new search engine that is advertised as the "world's first family-friendly Internet search site." We tried to locate information about 25 schools; 25 charitable and political organizations; 25 educational, artistic, and cultural institutions; and 25 concepts that might be of interest to young people. Our search terms included such phrases as the "American Red Cross," the "San Diego Zoo," and the "Smithsonian Institution," as well as such concepts as "Christianity," the "Bill of Rights" and "eating disorders." In every case in our sample, we found that the family-friendly search engine prevented us from obtaining access to almost 90 percent of the materials on the Internet containing the relevant search terms. We further found that in many cases, the search service denied access to 99 percent of material that would otherwise be available without the filters. We concluded that the filtering mechanism prevented children from obtaining a great deal of useful and appropriate information that is currently available on the Internet.

Introduction

The subject of whether to promote techniques to limit access to information available on the Internet grows out of the litigation against the Communications Decency Act. In that case, the Supreme Court ruled that the First Amendment protected the right to publish information on the Internet. The Court also found that "the interest in encouraging freedom of expression in a democratic society outweighs any theoretical but unproven benefit of censorship."

Shortly after the Supreme Court issued its decision, the White House convened a meeting to discuss the need to develop content filters for the Internet. The Administration unveiled a "Strategy for a Family Friendly Internet." According to the White House proposal, a key component would be the promotion of labeling and screening systems designed to shield children from inappropriate Internet content.

President Clinton said that he thought it was necessary to develop search engines specifically designed to screen out objectionable material. He said that it "must be our objective" to ensure that the labeling of Internet content "will become standard practice." Vice President Gore said, "Our challenge is to make these blocking technologies and the accompanying rating systems as common as the computers themselves."

In a statement released during the White House meeting, five Internet companies – CNET, Excite, Infoseek, Lycos and Yahoo! – expressed their support of the "White House proposal for the Internet industry to adopt a self-regulated rating system for content on the Web."

Following the White House summit, several companies announced that they would develop products and services for content filtering. On October 6, 1997, Net Shepherd and AltaVista launched Family Search. They described the product as "the world's first family-friendly Internet search site." Family Search is the first product to incorporate two of the goals identified at the July White House meeting – content rating and filtered search engines.

The "Family Search" Service

Net Shepherd Family Search is a web-based search engine located on the Internet at http://family.netshepherd.com. According to the "Frequently Asked Questions" (FAQ) file available at the site, Family Search "is designed to make the Internet a friendlier, more productive place for families. This is achieved though filtering out web sites judged by an independent panel of demographically appropriate Internet users, to be inappropriate and/or objectionable to average user families."

The Family Search service operates as follows: A user submits a search request, such as "American Red Cross." That request is then directed to the AltaVista search engine. The AltaVista results are then filtered through Net Shepherd's ratings database, and the filtered results are presented to the user. For this reason, conducting a search using the AltaVista search engine, and then conducting the same search using the Net Shepherd search engine, shows exactly how much information is removed by the Net Shepherd filter.

Net Shepherd claims that it has completed the most comprehensive rating of material on the World Wide Web. According to the company (as reported in the FAQ), in March of 1997 it had rated "97% of the English language sites on the Web."

For this survey, it is particularly important to emphasize two claims made by Net Shepherd about its family-friendly search engine. First, Net Shepherd states that the filtering criterion is whether a web site is "inappropriate and/or objectionable to average user families." Second, Net Shepherd states that its review of material available on the Web is comprehensive – "97% of the English language sites."

Survey Methodology

We set out to determine the actual effect of the filtering process – to quantify the amount of information that was actually blocked by a filtered search engine. Family Search's use of AltaVista results enabled us to conduct a straightforward comparison of a filtered and an unfiltered search. We first entered our search criteria into the AltaVista search engine [http://altavista.digital.com] and recorded the number of documents produced in reponse to our request. This number appeared at the top of search results returned by AltaVista.

We then duplicated our search request with Family Search and recorded the number of documents located through that search engine. Unlike AltaVista, Family Search does not report the number of matching documents. We had to read each page of the search results and manually count the number of documents retrieved.

All of our searches that contained more than one word in the search were submitted in quotation marks.

Family Search allows the user to designate a desired "quality" level for its search results. In conducting our searches, we used the default of "no preference." This is the most comprehensive setting and allowed us to retrieve all of the documents that Family Search would provide.

All of our searches were conducted between November 17 and November 26, 1997. We conducted 100 searches for key phrases using the unfiltered and the filtered search engines. We divided the 100 searches into four groups:

- Elementary, middle and high schools
- Charitable and political organizations
- Educational, artistic and cultural institutions
- Miscellaneous concepts and entities

We were particularly interested in the topics that would interest young people. For this reason we selected search phrases for organizations and ideas that we thought would be or should be of interest to children ages 18 and below. We are aware that not all families would agree that all of the phrases we selected would be appropriate for their children, but by and large we thought the 100 phrases we selected would likely be the types of searches that children who are using the Internet for non-objectionable purposes would conduct and that their parents would probably encourage.

Our findings are contained in the attached table. The results are summarized below:

Survey of Elementary, Middle and High Schools

With the growth of the Internet, many schools are today taking advantage of new communications technology. Not only are students able to access information around the world from a computer terminal in their classroom, they are also able to set up web sites. Many of these sites contain practical information – how to contact teachers, homework assignments, and cancellation policies. Many sites also include school projects. Although the content of the sites is as different as are the schools, one thing seems clear – the web sites in this category are web sites created for young people and often by young people. Thus when we tried locating these sites through the family-friendly search engine, we were surprised by the outcome.

The Arbor Heights Elementary School in Seattle, Washington maintains a highly regarded web site located at http://www.halcyon.com/arborhts/ arborhts.html. More than 70,000 people have visited the web site in the last two years. The school also publishes a magazine specifically for kids aged 7 through 12 called "Cool Writers Magazine" that is available at the web site.

If you go to the AltaVista search engine and search for "Arbor Heights Elementary," you will get back 824 hits. But if you use the Net Shepherd family-friendly search engine, only three documents are returned. In other words, Net Shepherd blocks access to more than 99 percent of the material that would otherwise be available on AltaVista containing the search phrase "Arbor Heights Elementary."

We found similar results with other searches. More than 96 percent of the material referring to "Providence School" is blocked by Family Search. Over 98 percent of the material referring to "Ralph Bunche School" is also blocked.

This seemed extraordinary to us. The blocking criteria deployed by Net Shepherd is, according to the company, whether a site is "inappropriate and/or objectionable to average user families." We looked at several of the pages that were returned with the unfiltered search engine but not with the filtered search engine. We could not find anything that an average user family would consider to be inappropriate or objectionable.

Survey of Charitable and Political Organizations

We selected 25 organizations representing national charities and groups across the political spectrum. Many of these organizations were established to provide services and assistance to children and parents. All have made important use of the Internet to provide timely and useful information on-line at little or no cost to families across the country.

The American Red Cross site (http://www.crossnet.org/), for example, provides an extraordinary collection of information about public health and medical resources. The American Red Cross has a special interest in families. It designated November "Child Safety and Protection Month." If you go to this web page [http://www.crossnet.org/healthtips/firstaid.html] you will find a special section devoted to "Health and Safety Tips: How to Protect Your Family with First Aid Training."

These resources and other similar materials are available if you conduct an AltaVista search for "American Red Cross." Almost 40,000 document were returned with the search. But a search with Family Search for the same phrase produced only 77 hits. The search engine filter had blocked access to 99.8

percent of the documents concerning the "American Red Cross" that would otherwise be available on the Internet.

Similar results were found when we conducted searches for the "Child Welfare League of America," "UNICEF" and "United Way."

Political organizations are also subject to extensive filtering. More than 4,000 documents about the NAACP can be found by means of AltaVista, but Family Search seems to believe that only 15 documents on the Internet concerning the NAACP are appropriate for young people.

Survey of Educational, Artistic and Cultural Institutions

Many organizations use the Internet today to provide all types of valuable information for young people. We conducted searches for many well known kids' activities, such as "Disneyland," "National Zoo," and the "Boy Scouts of America."

The National Aquarium in Baltimore is one of top attractions for young people in the mid-Atlantic region. The Aquarium has created an extensive web site [http://www.aqua.org/], filled with a lot of neat stuff. If you go to Think Tank, you can try to answer a daily question about aquatic life. In the Education section of the web site, titled "Wonder Leads to Understanding," you will learn more about special programs at the National Aquarium for young people. The Aquarium's resources are widely found across the Internet. An AltaVista search produced 2,134 responses. But the family-friendly search engine produced only 63 responses.

Intrigued by the tremendous discrepancy, we decided to visit every one of the first 200 web pages returned by Alta Vista to see how it could be that, on average, 97 percent of the material would be considered objectionable to the average user family. We did find several speeches and papers that mentioned the National Aquarium as well as several events that were held at the National Aquarium. We also learned that the United States does not have the only National Aquarium. Others can be found in Australia and the Phillipines. We learned that a few people take family pictures when they go to the National Aquarium and that people who work at the Aquarium mention it on their resumes. But we couldn't find any objectionable or inappropriate material.

For searches of information on the Internet on many of the most popular educational institutions in the United States for kids, Family Search routinely blocked 99 percent of the documents. "Yellowstone National Park" produced a blocking rate of 99.8 percent. The blocking rate for the "San Diego Zoo" was 99.6 percent.

One of the most peculiar results in the entire survey concerned our search for the "National Basketball Association." A straightforward search on AltaVista produced 18,018 hits. But when we tried Family Search, only two documents were provided. We have no idea what is in the remaining 18,016 documents that Family Search considers to be objectionable for the average family using the Internet.

Survey of Miscellaneous Concepts and Entities

For this last category, we considered the topics that students might be interested in learning more about as part of a school research paper or similar project. We tried to select concepts and entities from a range of areas appropriate for young people – science, history, geography, government, religion, as well as famous people.

Consider, for example, a young student who is writing a research paper on "Thomas Edison," one of the greatest inventors of all time. If the student undertakes a search with AltaVista, 11,522 documents are returned. But if the student uses the Family Search site, only nine documents are produced. Similar results will be found with such search phrases as "Betsy Ross," "Islam," "Emily Dickinson," and "United States Supreme Court."

We recognize that young people also have concerns about sensitive topics such as eating disorders, puberty, and teen pregnancy. Parents' views on how best to handle such issues varies considerably from family to family. Not surprisingly, most of the documents available on the Internet about these topics are extensively blocked by Family Search. But what was surprising to us is that the blocking of these sensitive matters was not any greater than with such topics as "photosynthesis" (99.5 percent), "astronomy" (99.9 percent) or "Wolfgang Amadeus Mozart" (99.9 percent). In other words, it is just as difficult to get information about the "Constitution of the United States" – actually, somewhat more so – as it is to get information about "puberty" using a family-friendly search engine.

Even Dr. Suess fares poorly with this family-friendly search engine. Only eight of the 2,638 references on the Internet relating to Dr. Suess are made available by Family Search. And one of the eight documents that was produced by the search engine turned out to be a parody of a Dr. Suess story using details from the murder of Nicole Brown Simpson.

Limitations of Survey

We recognized in the course of the survey a number of limitations on our survey method. First, the figures that we provide regarding how much material the search engine blocks actually represent a percentage of the information blocked that would otherwise be available by means of the AltaVista search engine. There is material available on the Internet that is not located by AltaVista, but could be found by other locator services such as Yahoo! or Hotbot. If this factor were taken into account, the percentage of materials blocked by Family Search, expressed as a percentage of all the material available on the Internet containing the relevant search phrases, would necessarily increase.

We also recognize that there is some ambiguity in search terms and that context is often necessary to establish meaning. We tried where possible to select search terms that would reduce the risk of ambiguity.

W did not attempt to review all of the filtering products currently available. For the reasons described above, and particularly the emphasis that filter proponents have placed on search engines that can perform this task, we believed it was appropriate to limit our study to the one search engine specifically designed to block access to "inappropriate material."

Conclusion

Our research showed that a family-friendly search engine, of the kind recommended by proponents of Internet rating schemes at the White House summit in July 1997, typically blocked acccess to 95-99 percent of the material available on the Internet that might be of interest to young people. We also found that as information on popular topics became more widely available on the Internet, the search engine was likely to block an even higher percentage. We further found that the search engine did not seem to restrict sensitive topics for young people any more than it restricted matters of general interest. Even with the very severe blocking criteria employed, we noted that some material which parents might consider to be objectionable was still provided by the family-friendly service.

Our review led us to conclude that proponents of filters and rating systems should think more carefully about whether this is a sensible approach. In the end, "family-friendly" filtering does not seem very friendly.

Recommendations

While it is true that there is material available on the Internet that some will find legitimately objectionable, it is also clear that in some cases the proposed solutions may be worse than the actual problem. Filtering programs that deny children access to a wide range of useful and appropriate materials ultimately diminish the educational value of the Internet.

> The White House should reconsider its support for the Internet filtering effort, and particularly for the idea of filter-based search engines. This approach is flawed and these programs make it more difficult for young people to find useful and appropriate information.

> Vendors of filtering and tagging products need to be much more forthcoming about the actual effect of their programs and services. It is deceptive and fraudulent to say that a program blocks "objectionable content" when it also blocks a great deal of information that is useful and valuable for young people.

> Alternatives to software filters and tagging should be explored. The European Union has recently proposed a range of options including codes of conduct, hotlines, and warnings.

> Parents should learn more about the benefits of the Internet for their children and families. In the ongoing debate about the availability of objectionable materials, one key point has been lost – the Internet is a wonderful resource for young people.

> Parents should continue to take a strong interest in their children's use of the Internet. Helping children tell right from wrong is not something that should be left to computer software or search engines.

We hope that additional research will be done on the impact other filtering programs may have on the ability of young people to obtain useful information on the Internet. Without such studies, it is not possible to say whether it is sensible to promote these programs.

Resources

Internet Free Expression Alliance [http://www.ifea.net/] – IFEA was established to protect the free flow of information on the Internet. It includes more than two dozen member organizations. Information is available from the IFEA web site about rating and filtering systems, including the views of the American Civil Liberties Union, the American Library Association, the Computer Professionals for Social Responsibility, the Electronic Frontier Foundation, the Electronic Privacy Information Center, the National Campaign for Freedom of Expression, the National Coalition Against Censorship, and others.

About EPIC

The Electronic Privacy Information Center is a public interest research organization, based in Washington, DC.

Electronic Privacy Information Center 666 Pennsylvania Ave., SE Suite 301 Washington, DC 20003 +1 202 544 9240 (tel) +1 202 547 5482 (fax) http://www.epic.org/

Appendix – Tables of Search Results

Table 1: Elementary, Middle and High Schools

Search Terms	Hits: AltaVista	Hits: Family Search	Percent Filtered
Arbor Heights Elementary	824	3	99.6%*
Avocado Elementary School	181	26	85.6%
Biboohra State School	35	2	94.2%
Camp Creek Elementary School	83	9	89.1%
Clearview Elementary School	94	10	89.3%
Evergreen Elementary School	210	12	94.2%
Frenchtown School	69	1	98.5%
Grace Church School	67	6	91.0%
Hillside Elementary	1737	20	98.8%
Keolu Elementary School	48	4	91.6%
Marshall Elementary School	465	15	96.7%
New Hope Elementary School	71	5	92.9%
Oak Hill Academy	492	16	96.7%
Providence Day School	241	9	96.2%
Ralph Bunche School	981	14	98.5%
Riverdale School	446	25	94.3%
Shady Hill School	191	16	91.6%
St. Therese School	160	7	95.6%
University Park Elementary	575	11	98.0%
Woodward Avenue Elementary School	92	2	97.8%
Vista Middle School	647	13	97.9%
Trinity Christian School	377	17	95.4%
Claremont High School	773	8	98.9%
Los Alamos High School	609	15	97.5%
Westview Centennial Secondary School	89	2	97.7%

Table 2: Charitable and/or Political Organizations

Search Terms	Hits: AltaVista	Hits: Family Search	Percent Filtered
American Association of Retired Persons	8498	25	99.7%
American Cancer Society	38762	6	99.9%
American Family Association	3335	12	99.6%
American Red Cross	39434	77	99.8%
Catholic Relief Services	1777	18	98.9%
Child Welfare League of America	2170	19	99.9%
Christian Coalition	16170	19	99.8%
Concerned Women for America	2182	23	98.9%
Congress of National Black Churches	282	27	90.4%
Cystic Fibrosis Foundation	2830	15	99.4%
Family Friendly Libraries	181	20	88.9%
Family Research Council	4286	32	99.2%
Focus on the Family	6172	23	99.6%
Hostelling International American Youth Hostels	374	10	99.7%
Klaas Foundation	933	64	93.1%
Leukemia Society of America	2723	13	99.5%
National Association for the Advancement of Colored People	4076	15	99.6%
National Association of Homes and Services for Children	135	7	94.8%
National Consumers League	1692	10	99.4%
National Organization for Women	8270	35	99.5%
National Rifle Association	11828	19	99.8%
UNICEF	1423	17	98.8%
United Cerebral Palsy Association	941	21	97.7%
United Jewish Appeal	3024	1	99.9%
United Way	54300	23	99.9%

Table 3: Educational, Artistic and/or Cultural Institutions

Search Terms	Hits: AltaVista	Hits: Family Search	Percent Filtered
Art Institute of Chicago	9785	10	99.9%
Boy Scouts of America	22297	35	99.8%
Carnegie Library	5755	32	99.4%
Cleveland Orchestra	2689	18	99.3%
Dance Theater of Harlem	317	27	91.4%
Disneyland	11129	31	99.7%
Folger Shakespeare Library	1421	18	98.7%
Future Farmers of America	2205	22	99.0%
Future Homemakers of America	1280	12	99.0%
Girl Scouts of America	1606	30	98.1%
Grand Old Opry	371	31	91.6%
Independence Hall	3281	22	99.3%
Julliard School of Music	500	11	97.8%
Kennedy Center	13068	71	99.4%
Metropolitan Museum of Art	19930	50	99.7%
Museum of Modern Art	23566	31	99.8%
National Aquarium	2134	63	97.0%
National Basketball Association	18018	2	99.9%
National Gallery of Art	8655	73	99.1%
National Zoo	4142	6	99.8%
Public Broadcasting System	3603	26	99.2%
Radio City Music Hall	5594	20	99.6%
San Diego Zoo	5895	21	99.6%
Smithsonian Institution	51033	37	99.9%
Yellowstone National Park	14933	26	99.8%

Table 4: Miscellaneous Concepts or Entities (potential research topics)

Search Terms	Hits: AltaVista	Hits: Family Search	Percent Filtered
Astronomy	121306	22	99.9%
Betsy Ross	3055	23	99.2%
Bill of Rights	46195	44	99.9%
Catholicism	4590	12	99.7%
Christianity	37574	13	99.9%
Christopher Columbus	13498	5	99.9%
Constitution of the United States	17877	31	99.8%
Democratic Party	56333	22	99.9%
Dr. Suess	2638	8	99.6%
Eating Disorders	11602	23	99.8%
Emily Dickinson	10050	8	99.9%
First Amendment	58529	94	99.8%
Frederick Douglass	7286	24	99.6%
House of Representatives	158972	38	99.9%
Islam	27572	10	99.9%
Judaism	11985	7	99.9%
Photosynthesis	4963	23	99.5%
Puberty	2276	25	98.9%
Republican Party	28218	21	99.9%
Romeo and Juliet	24428	47	99.8%
Teen pregnancy	13113	46	99.6%
Thomas Edison	11522	9	99.9%
U.S. Senate	18810	41	99.7%
United States Supreme Court	19917	20	99.9%
Wolfgang Amadeus Mozart	7074	7	99.9%

* All percentages have been rounded down to the nearest tenth of a percent.

Censored Internet Access in Utah Public Schools and Libraries

The Censorware Project

Abstract

The Utah Education Network (www.uen.org) is an agency of the Utah state government charged with providing telecommunications services, including internet access, to public schools and libraries in Utah. UEN uses a commercial software package to censor the internet access of all of the 40 school districts and at least eight of the 70 library districts in Utah.

An examination of the results of this censoring during the period September 10-October 10, 1998, found that many users were banned from accessing sites useful for educational and research purposes. Banned accesses made up less than 1% of overall accesses, most of which were banner ads presumed (by the software) to be sexually explicit. Very few people used the internet to access sexually explicit material, and students were the least likely to do so. It thus appears that the stated problem of minors accessing sexually explicit material (inadvertently or deliberately) is considerably less than some organizations would have the public and the Congress believe.

UEN censors many things that are not in any way illegitimate for Utah adults or students to view. Among the documents which UEN prevented citizens from viewing:

- The Declaration of Independence
- The United States Constitution

Written by Michael Sims with Bennett Haselton, Jamie McCarthy, James S. Tyre, Jonathan Wallace, David Smith and Gabriel Wachob (Version 1.1, March 1999). The complete text of this report, including detailed charts and appendices, is available at The Censorware Project's website: http://censorware.org/reports/utah/.

- The Bible
- The Book of Mormon
- The Koran
- The Adventures of Sherlock Holmes
- A Connecticut Yankee in King Arthur's Court
- George Washington's Farewell Address
- The Mayflower Compact
- All of Shakespeare's plays
- The Canterbury Tales
- Wuthering Heights
- "Marijuana: Facts for Teens" (a U.S. Government brochure)

as well as many others, including safe-sex sites, sites discussing AIDS prevention, magazines available at any newsstand (Glamour, Seventeen), etc.

Statistics on the banning are presented, with a discussion of the results.

Introduction

In April 1998, the Salt Lake Tribune, a Utah newspaper, ran a story entitled "Web Sex Sites: Public School Logs Show Denied Hits." The story was picked up by the Associated Press and eventually ran in a number of newspapers nationwide. The story indicated, among other things, that the Utah Education Network, which provides internet access for essentially all Utah public schools and many libraries, kept log files of the internet accesses made through their service and employed a software censoring product, Smartfilter, to censor internet access at schools and libraries. (Smartfilter is a product of Secure Computing Corporation, http://www.securecomputing.com/).The Censorware Project and David Smith decided to request these log files under Utah's Government Records Access and Management Act (known as GRAMA, this is Utah's "Freedom of Information" act).

Internet access in schools and libraries is a hot topic. And there is a great lack of hard data about it. We hope this report (and the accompanying data, which is also available) will begin to fill that void.

Obtaining the files was easier decided upon than accomplished. UEN refused to provide these public records, and under GRAMA, we appealed to the Utah State Records Committee. UEN's cited reasons included an invasion of privacy of the users of the system, although many administrators have access to these computer log files and UEN specifically bans websites which users could use to protect their privacy on-line. In June 1998, after a hearing on the issue, the State Records Committee ordered UEN to provide the files. To eliminate any question of invading the privacy of the users, all of the originating internet addresses were redacted. The log files as presented represent an anonymous picture of the aggregate usage of UEN's network.

In July 1998, UEN decided not to appeal the decision of the State Records Committee and offered a set of the log files. UEN had flouted Utah state law by destroying the log files from April - May 1998, which we had requested, and instead offered the current files from July, when school was not in session and the log files were therefore much less useful. We complained to the State Records Committee, which took a step it had never before taken: they recommended the matter to the Salt Lake County District Attorney, Neal Gunnarson, for investigation and possible prosecution.

Mr. Gunnarson, who achieved fame in 1997 by getting caught destroying copies of a Utah newspaper which he took exception to, failed to investigate or take any action against UEN. The complaint was promptly buried and forgotten, proving that no matter what the law says, and no matter how blatant the violation, if the will to enforce it is not present, the law is worthless.

Since the original log files had been destroyed, we decided to get a set of files from September 1998, when school would be in session. We obtained them, with much better cooperation from UEN this time, and after some delays, produced the following report.

Methodology, Background and Sample Population

Log files created by UEN's eleven proxy servers running the Smartfilter software were collected and analyzed. A "proxy server" is a computer through which requests for documents on the internet pass. The software running on the proxy server examines each request as it is made and decides whether to accept it (and fetch the requested document) or reject it. The decision is made by consulting an encrypted list of internet addresses which were determined, by Secure Computing Corporation, to fall into one of 27 categories. When the access is accepted or rejected, the proxy servers note the result in an electronic log file.

The log files covered the period 10 September through 10 October 1998, inclusive, which represented 20 days when school was in session and 11 non-school days. The files contained the following information:

IP address of accessing computer [REDACTED by UEN]
Date/time of access
Method of access
URL accessed
HTTP specification
HTTP status code
Number of bytes returned
Smartfilter category classification

The log files ended up being 838 Mb compressed; approximately 6.5 Gigabytes uncompressed, and included about 53 million lines of data, with each line representing one access or attempted access of a resource on the World Wide Web. Email, chat (except for web-based chat), and other methods of using the internet are not covered by these log files and are not known to be intercepted by Smartfilter.

The log files were not pristine. Files from the various proxy servers were combined into a single file for transmission to us. When received, they contained inconsistencies, especially in the places where one file ended and the next began. A very small number of URLs were discarded due to these errors in the files. This is not expected to bias the results in any measurable fashion.

The files were scanned by a custom-written computer program (perl), which collected statistics about the files and separated the URLs by which category(ies) they were banned under. Smartfilter classifies documents on the web into 27 categories, any or all of which can be activated by the entity controlling the software (UEN). UEN has five of the 27 categories activated: "Sex," "Gambling," "Criminal Skills," "Hate Speech," and "Drugs." A URL can be classified in multiple categories. If a user tries to access a URL which is classified in any of the five categories which UEN has activated, they will generally receive a message saying that access has been denied.

Certain statistics regarding the files were also collected with image files excluded, to the extent possible. For these statistics, URLs ending in "gif" or "jpg" or "jpeg" were excluded, as well as all URLs from domains known to be dedicated to serving banner ads. This process is slightly overinclusive – if a user visited the banner ad domain directly, to look up advertising rates for example, these accesses would be discarded. It is also moderately underinclusive – there are sites which serve image files in various non-standard methods,which would not be caught nor discarded by this procedure.

UEN has no access to Smartfilter's list of banned sites. They will know a given site is banned only by attempting to access it and being blocked from doing so. UEN does not make additions to the list of banned sites and makes very few removals (see discussion). For all practical purposes, the makers of Smartfilter (Secure Computing Corporation of San Jose, California) make the final decisions as to what Utah students, adults and library patrons can view over the internet.

Costs to UEN for maintaining the censoring proxy servers are significant. A newspaper article indicated the cost for the software alone is approximately $20,000 per year. UEN's budget for fiscal year 1999 indicates they were allocated $12,000 for proxy software and $124,048 for proxy hardware. There are also substantial costs associated with the personnel to maintain and administer these servers.

After the files were scanned and separated into categories, the URLs which had been banned in each category were reviewed. For the four smaller categories, this review was simply scanning over the list looking for URLs which seemed "out of place." For the "Sex" category, another script (computer program) was employed to aid in the review. URLs which appeared to represent valuable resources wrongly or irrationally banned were called up (see discussion). The review process likely missed many such URLs. The review process should have been efficient enough to discover the majority (>50%; perhaps >75%) of the wrongful bans present in the log files. Note that this applies only to the list of wrongly or irrationally banned sites at the end of the report; the statistics and graphs presented were compiled by a simple computer program and are presumed to be 100% accurate. Achieving 100% accuracy in reviewing the banned sites would require humans to examine the document at every URL banned, which is prohibitively difficult.

The user population which created these log files is diverse. During school days, the users are predominantly public school students. The vast majority of Utah public schools are wired for internet access (although sometimes this means having one computer with a modem); a majority of the wired schools have computing facilities available to students. In general, it appears that many Utah high schools are well-connected and have multiple computers available to students, while many elementary schools may have only a single computer with a dial-up connection to the internet, which may be available only for class demonstrations and the like and not for student use. It is assumed that the bulk of student internet accesses are from students aged 13-18. From information provided by UEN and our own research, it is believed that all public elementary and secondary schools in Utah have all of their internet access provided through UEN's Smartfilter-equipped proxy servers.

According to the Census Bureau, Utah has some 500,000 residents between the ages of 5 and 17. Not all of them attend public schools; there are approximately 30 private schools plus the possibility of home schooling. Considering this factor and the factors listed previously, we believe a reasonable estimate for the number of public school students who had the opportunity to use the internet during the sampled time period to be in the neighborhood of 100,000-150,000. We have no estimate for the number of library patrons and dial-up educators whose accesses contribute to the non-school day logs.

During non-school days, the users are predominantly library patrons, with a smattering of dial-up users (these people would also be present during the school days, of course, and make up a sort of "background" presence to the scholastic users). UEN provides dial-up access at all hours of the day and night to an unknown number of teachers statewide. Thus, accesses which occur at times when neither libraries or schools are open are from these dial-up services. Of the 70 public library systems in Utah, at least eight use UEN's proxy servers, and probably several more. A few public libraries in Utah use other censoring software products. Many public libraries do not censor internet access. Urban areas may be less likely to have censored internet access than rural areas. Nationally, the average age of internet users is 30-35, so this population can probably be assumed to be significantly older than the student population.

Internet usage during school days is approximately 20 times that of non-school days.

Discussion

The results show that only a small percentage of the URLs accessed were banned by Smartfilter. Overall, approximately 0.39% of all accesses were stopped by the program. Additionally, there were substantial differences in the access patterns between the times when school was in session and when it was not. (The distinction between school and non-school days is crucial. See Methodology for more information.)

Overall, about one out of every 260 requests was banned. For school days, the figure was lower: about one out of every 280 requests. For days when school was not in session, the figure was twice as high: about one out of every 120 requests was censored. One can view this in two ways: high school students are much less likely to access banned material, or adults are more likely to.

Tables 1 and 2. Overall Statistics

Time Period	Total Accesses	Total Banned Accesses	Sex	Drugs	Hate Speech	Criminal Skills	Gambling
All days	53,103,387	205,737	193,272	1,588	791	4,934	5,772
All School Days	50,461,490	182,600	171,509	1,557	762	4,440	5,129
All Non-School Days	2,641,897	23,137	21,763	31	29	494	643

Time Period	Total Accesses (%)	Total Banned Accesses (%)	Sex (%)	Drugs (%)	Hate Speech (%)	Criminal Skills (%)	Gambling (%)
All days	100	0.387	0.364	0.0030	0.0015	0.0093	0.011
All School Days	100	0.362	0.340	0.0031	0.0015	0.0088	0.010
All Non-School Days	100	0.876	0.824	0.0012	0.0011	0.019	0.024

During the examination, it became apparent that many of the accesses which were being banned, primarily in the "Sex" category, were banner ads. Some websites include banner ads which are sent from other sites, internet advertising companies which send out hundreds of thousands of banner ads daily. Smartfilter was banning many of these banner ad sites under its "Sex" category, possibly because some of them displayed banner ads on sexually-explicit websites or displayed sexually-explicit banner ads. This seemed to considerably inflate the number of banned accesses under the "Sex" category, because someone could be visiting, say, Yahoo.com, and if Yahoo was using one of the banned banner ad sites, each page visited on Yahoo would lead to another entry in the logfiles as the banner ad was rejected. Thus it is entirely possible to generate banned accesses in these log files when the user never intended to visit any sort of sexually-explicit site (see also the discussion of wrongly banned sites).

In order to examine this situation, we resolved to examine the log files without counting images. It is important to understand the procedure that occurs when one accesses a web page:

Situation A. Load a page. The HTML file (the text on the page) is loaded first. It may reference anywhere from zero to hundreds of images in its code. When the HTML page is loaded, the individual images are then loaded. The total number of accesses is equal to one for the HTML page plus one for each image loaded.

Situation B. Load a page. The page is banned by Smartfilter and rejected. No images are loaded. The total number of accesses is one.

Thus, eliminating images from consideration effectively normalizes the distribution: accessing one page, whether it is banned or not, counts as one access. We felt this might be a more useful tally (although of course the straight access count is valid as well).

We undertook to exclude all images from the logfiles and recompile the statistics on a no-images basis. (See the Methodology for more information.) The results were roughly as expected. Eliminating the images eliminated very many of the overall hits, more than two-thirds. The percentage of bans was therefore increased across the board, although the number of banned hits dropped as well with the elimination of the images. The "Sex" category showed the greatest drop: almost half of the "Sex" accesses were eliminated, showing that very many of the original "Sex" bans were not caused by people looking for pornography but were banner ads, probably completely innocent, that were served from banned domains.

Tables 3 and 4. Statistics Excluding Images and Known Banner-Ad Sites

Time Period	Total Accesses	Total Banned Accesses	Sex	Drugs	Hate Speech	Criminal Skills	Gambling
All days	15,434,442	95,059	86,957	1,298	526	3,753	3,649
All School Days	14,462,434	83,503	76,267	1,273	498	3,383	3,111
All Non-School Days	972,008	11,556	10,690	25	28	370	538

Time Period	Total Accesses (%)	Total Banned Accesses (%)	Sex (%)	Drugs (%)	Hate Speech (%)	Criminal Skills (%)	Gambling (%)
All days	100's	0.616	0.563	0.0084	0.0034	0.024	0.024
All School Days	100	0.577	0.527	0.0088	0.0034	0.023	0.022
All Non-School Days	100	1.189	1.100	0.0026	0.0029	0.038	0.055

Examination of the log files also showed that late-night (i.e., adult) accesses were much more likely to be banned. Graphs of these data (available at http://www.censorware.org/reports/utah/charts.shtml) relate the time of day and whether it was a school or non-school day to the number of accesses and number of bans recorded at that time. The charts also include a category called "universal," which is shorthand for sites which are banned under *all* of Smartfilter's categories. These universal bans are on sites which might allow someone to get around the banning, such as www.anonymizer.com.

Figures 1-4 show total statistics. Both charts showing total accesses (Fig. 1,3) show a very pronounced "bell" shape, having many more accesses occurring during the middle of the day. The curves for banned accesses (Fig. 2,4) show somewhat flatter shapes, as more of the bans occur in the evenings and late nights. Figures 5-8 show the same statistics with images removed. These graphs are much flatter, especially the graphs of banned sites. The fact that removing banned images flattens the graphs shows that more of the "unintentional," banner-ad bans occurred during the day while accesses at night were less likely to be of this variety. Generally, school accesses which generated "Sex" bans were more likely to be "innocent" than accesses attributable to library or dial-up usage.

Wrongful Bans

Wrongful bans are another important part of the equation. The Appendix to this paper includes a listing of sites which some Utah resident attempted to access and which were censored, during September 10-October 10. It is important to note that these represent real people being banned from real sites - the document at the banned URL is described underneath the URL. Each URL listed was banned at least once during the sample period. Many URLs were attempted to be accessed many times, but are listed only once in the listing. In many cases, to avoid boring the reader, we have listed only one URL from a site even though many URLs from that site were attempted to be accessed and banned.

Wrongful bans are listed in the Appendix. Some interesting evidence turns up upon scrutiny of them. Secure Computing states:

> As a rule, sites are not added to the Control List without first being viewed and approved by our staff.

There is a great deal of evidence that this is untrue. Offspring.com is banned under the Criminal Skills category for lyrics which use phrases like "crack the codes," "tap" and "surveillance" – but it's a rock group, not a site discussing "Criminal Skills." A website about a computer game named "Grand Theft Auto" is banned for its "Criminal Skills." A scholarly paper about Nazi Germany is banned, as well as sites which *oppose* hate speech and racism. National Families in Action and the Life Education Network, two groups which oppose drug abuse, are banned. A music group called "Bud Good and the Goodbuds" is banned under Drugs, for obvious reasons. An appeals court decision in a drug case is banned under Drugs. The Iowa State Division of Narcotics Enforcement is banned. A government brochure put out by the National Institute of Health is banned under Drugs. It is entitled "Marijuana: Facts for Teens." A page at Florida State University is banned under Gambling:

http://mailer.fsu.edu/~wwager/index_public.html

Look carefully at that URL. Do you see the phrase "wwager" in it? The author of the page is named Walter Wager. That is why this page was banned under Gambling – because a computer, not a human, read that page and decided that since it involved "wager"ing, it should be categorized under Gambling. Similarly, a computer can read a page which uses the word "Narcotics," and, not realizing that it's the Iowa State Police, adds it to the list.

These are the sorts of mistakes computers make. Companies that make censoring software employ computers to search through the world wide web looking for materials which meet their criteria. A computer sees a page which uses the phrase "grand theft auto," and decides immediately that this must involve Criminal Skills, and adds the page immediately to the list of banned sites. No human would decide that the page for a computer game involved Criminal Skills, but a computer easily could. Nor would a page written by Walter Wager be classified under Gambling by a human - but a computer might.

Secure Computing states that every site on their list was examined by a human before being added to the blacklist. (UEN, in a report to their superiors during the implementation of the Smartfilter system, stated that "[Smartfilter] uses *educators* to evaluate if the site is appropriate or not," emphasis added, although this is not and has never been true.) In fact, the most likely case is that humans may be employed to supervise and monitor the computers, and make some decisions about banning some sites, but that the computer program itself also adds sites to the blacklist on its own initiative. This is a cost-effective way to deal with the 500,000,000 or so web pages available over the internet, and since few customers will discover the errors that it creates, companies which make censoring software will be tempted to delegate more and more responsibility to computer programs. The Censorware Project has examined many different censorware products and to date, all of them have exhibited characteristics which indicated that the companies involved were lying about employing humans and humans alone to add sites to the list. Companies are unwilling to take the public relations hit that would come from admitting that computers perform the selection of "bad" sites, but they are also unwilling to take the financial hit from hiring the hundreds or thousands of humans it would take to have a chance at keeping up with the internet's rate of change and growth.

The other interesting factor disclosed by the wrongful bans is the ban on candyland.com. This site resolves to the corporate homepage of Hasbro, the toymaker (who owns the rights to the board game Candy Land). Originally owned by a porn site, this domain was sued by Hasbro in 1996 and forced to stop using it in, if our information is correct, February 1996. They took all content off the site and for a while it was simply empty. It formally turned over to Hasbro in March 1997. Therefore, Smartfilter has not reviewed this site since at least March 1997, and more probably since 1996, because any recent review would have found no content or Hasbro instead of porn. This provides a good indication as to how frequently sites are re-reviewed for changed content - most likely, they are never re-reviewed. Candyland.com will stay banned as a porn site indefinitely (or until Secure Computing reads this report), although it has had no pornography for more than two years, because the constant growth of the internet requires censorware companies to spend their time searching for new sites, not reviewing old sites already on their blacklist. Over time, this will also lead to substantial errors as domains and individual users turn over, change content, etc.

Overridden Bans

UEN has the capability to override bans of certain sites. If a site comes to UEN's attention which should not be banned, yet is, UEN can enter this site into the software and allow it to be accessed. UEN puts several barriers in the way of actually implementing this, though; appeals regarding banned sites must run through the scholastic chain of command, through the school principal and district supervisor. Obviously few teachers or other persons encountering a wrongly banned site would pursue this, and this is shown by the extremely few number of sites which UEN has bothered to override from the default blacklist presented to them by Secure Computing. The following sites showed up as overridden in the log files:

> **http://209.75.21.6/**
> This is a company which serves banner ads.

> **http://www.mormon.com/**
> All things Mormon. Currently banned under Sex, but overridden. [Not entirely, see further discussion.]

> **http://fafsaws1.fafsa.ed.gov/**
> The Free Application for Federal Student Aid, a form which is required to be filed for all applicants for college financial aid.

http://netaddress.usa.net/

Free web-based email service. Currently banned under Chat (thus, not banned under UEN's settings, but obviously was at some time.)

http://www.cyberteens.com/

Stories and whatnot, by and for teenagers. Like mormon.com, this site has both banned and unbanned accesses.

http://www.infoseek.com/

All ads at Infoseek (http://www.infoseek.com/ads/) are banned under the Sex category. This was apparently causing some problems, or perhaps all of Infoseek was banned, so this override was placed.

Mormon.com and cyberteens.com are the most interesting. Both of these sites have instances in the log files where they are banned, and instances where they are permitted to be accessed due to an override placed by UEN. It is our suspicion that UEN attempted to override the bans on these sites, but did not do so for all of the eleven proxy servers – thus, in some areas of Utah, students attempting to access mormon.com will be banned from doing so and in some areas they will be allowed. Neither mormon.com nor cyberteens.com has any material inappropriate for teenagers.

Previous Evaluations

It is difficult to compare these statistics to past performance, in Utah or elsewhere, as this is the first comprehensive evaluation of censoring software performance in real-life conditions. (Documentation relating to the lawsuit filed in Loudoun County, Virginia, provides the second-best source of such information; available online at http://censorware.org/legal/ loudoun/). A document written in November 1996, just after UEN began using Smartfilter, indicates that "less than 0.7%" of all accesses were banned at that time. During the intervening two years to September 1998, gross accesses have increased by 1300% and the percentage of accesses banned has decreased somewhat to approximately 0.4% (see previous tables). Another document from March 1998 indicates that at that time, 0.60% of all accesses were banned. Although UEN states that they undertake to evaluate the effectiveness and performance of the censoring software they use, they were unable to provide any documentation of ever having done so beyond compiling gross statistics on the number and percentage of accesses banned, which their software does automatically.

It is perhaps worth noting that when UEN began providing internet access to Utah schools, the original plan was to allow each school district to create their own list of sites which they did not wish to be accessible over the internet, and for UEN to enforce these lists for each district. If they had implemented that plan, it is likely that documents such as the U.S. Constitution and Declaration of Independence would not today be banned in Utah.

Conclusion

When the Declaration of Independence is banned from the citizens of Saudi Arabia, so that they won't get ideas, we call it culturally backward. And when it's banned from our own public libraries by our own government, then what do we call it?

Readers who skim the Appendix will note that the entire Internet Wiretap server (wiretap.area.com or wiretap.spies.com) is banned under the Criminal Skills category. The archive contains hundreds of megabytes of books out of copyright, governmental and civics material, religious material, etc. What got it banned might have been the statement on its opening page, which a computer routine probably considered to be indicative of bomb-making:

Wiretap's Inspiration
The First Amendment

"Congress shall make no law respecting an establishment of religion, or prohibiting the free exercise thereof; or abridging the freedom of speech, or of the press; or the right of the people peaceably to assemble, and to petition the Government for a redress of grievances."

Disturbed by free speech?

"Printer's ink has been running a race against gunpowder these many, many years. Ink is handicapped, in a way, because you can blow up a man with gunpowder in half a second, while it may take twenty years to blow him up with a book. But the gunpowder destroys itself along with its victim, while a book can keep on exploding for centuries."

Christopher Morley, "The Haunted Bookshop"

It is a sad day when a quotation about free speech can get hundreds of books banned without any public oversight or review. UEN, in its quest to eliminate so-called undesirable content, has instead eliminated the one thing that makes the United States different and better than other countries around the world: the ability for citizens to speak and read freely, without the government watching over your shoulder.

Acknowledgements

Special thanks to –

Seth Finkelstein, who provided valuable technical assistance in obtaining and dealing with the log files; Joel Campbell, Freedom of Information Chairman of the Utah Chapter of the Society of Professional Journalists; The Utah State Records Committee, especially Chairman Max Evans; Chip Ward, on the Utah Library Association's Intellectual Freedom Committee; Ethel Jacob, Head Graphing Consultant for this report; and of course to UEN, without whom none of this would have been possible (or necessary).

Filtering FAQ

Computer Professionals for Social Responsibility

Introduction

Seen by some as a powerful tool for protecting children from online pornography and by others as "censorware," Internet content filters have generated much controversy, debate, and confusion.

This document attempts to describe the concerns and issues raised by the various types of filtering software. It is hoped that these questions and answers will help parents, libraries, schools, and others understand the software that they may be considering (or using).

Additions, clarifications, and corrections regarding the content of this document will be most graciously accepted: please send email to hhochheiser@cpsr.org.

1) Basics

1.1) What is a content filter?

A content filter is one or more pieces of software that work together to prevent users from viewing material found on the Internet. This process has two components.

Rating: Value judgments are used to categorize web sites based on their content. These ratings could use simple allowed/disallowed distinctions like those found in programs like CyberSitter or NetNanny, or they can have many values, as seen in ratings systems based on Platform for Internet Content Selection (PICS, see question 3.0).

The CPSR Filtering FAQ was prepared by Harry Hochheiser. Version 1.1.1. Last modified 2/14/98. http://www.cpsr.org//filters/faq.html.

Filtering: With each request for information, the filtering software examines the resource that the user has requested. If the resource is on the "not allowed" list, or if it does not have the proper PICS rating, the filtering software tells the user that access has been denied and the browser does not display the contents of the web site.

The first content filters were stand-alone systems consisting of mechanisms for determining which sites should be blocked, along with software to do the filtering, all provided by a single vendor.

The other type of content filter is protocol-based. These systems consist of software that uses established standards for communicating ratings information across the Internet. Unlike stand-alone systems, protocol-based systems do not contain any information regarding which sites (or types of sites) should be blocked. Protocol-based systems simply know how to find this information on the Internet, and how to interpret it.

1.2) Why do many people want filtering?

The Internet contains a wide range of materials, some of which may be offensive or even illegal in many countries. Unlike traditional media, the Internet does not have any obvious tools for segregating material based on content. While pornographic magazines can be placed behind the counter of a store, and strip-tease joints restricted to certain parts of town, the Internet provides everything through the same medium.

Filters and ratings systems are seen as tools that would provide the cyberspace equivalent of the physical separations that are used to limit access to "adult" materials. In rating a site as objectionable, and refusing to display it on the user's computer screen, filters and ratings systems can be used to prevent children from seeing material that their parents find objectionable. In preventing access, the software acts as an automated version of the convenience-store clerk who refuses to sell adult magazines to high-school students.

Filters are also used by businesses to prevent employees from accessing Internet resources that are either not work related or otherwise deemed inappropriate.

1.3) Can filtering programs be turned off?

It is assumed that parents or other authoritative users who install filtering programs would control the passwords that allow the programs to be disabled. This means that parents can enable the filter for their children but disable it for themselves. As with all other areas of computer security, these programs are vulnerable to attack by clever computer users who may be able to guess the password or to disable the program by other means.

1.4) I don't want to filter, but I do want to know what my child is viewing. Is that possible?

Some products include a feature that will capture the list of all Internet sites that have been visited from your computer. This allows a parent to see what sites their child has viewed, albeit after the fact. Similar software allows employers to monitor the Internet use of their employees. Users of these systems will not know that their Internet use is being watched unless they are explicitly told.

Whether used in homes or workplaces, these tools raise serious privacy concerns.

1.5) What is the scope of Internet content filtering? Do filters cover the WWW? Newsgroups? IRC? Email?

While some stand-alone systems claim to filter other parts of the Internet, most content filters are focused on the World-Wide-Web. Given the varied technical nature of the protocols involved, it's likely that filtering tools will do well with some of these, and poorly with others. For example, filtering software can easily block access to newsgroups with names like "alt.sex". However, current technology cannot identify the presence of explicit photos in a file that's being transferred via FTP. PICS-based systems currently only filter web sites.

2) Stand-alone Systems

2.1) What is a stand-alone system?

A stand-alone filtering system is a complete filtering solution provided by a single vendor. These filters block sites based on criteria provided by the software vendor, thus "locking in" users. If a customer does not like the vendor's selection of sites that are to be blocked, she must switch to a different software product.

2.2) Who decides what gets blocked and what doesn't?

This is the biggest practical difference between stand-alone systems and protocol-based systems. Stand-alone systems limit users to decisions made by the software vendor, although some let the parents or installers add and remove sites. Protocol-based systems provide users with a choice between alternative ratings systems, which publishers and third parties can use to develop ratings for content. See question 3.2 for more information.

2.3) How do stand-alone programs determine what should be blocked?

Currently available filtering tools use some combination of two approaches to evaluate content: lists of unacceptable (or acceptable) sites, and keyword searches.

List-based blocking works by explicitly enumerating sites that should either be blocked or allowed. These lists are generally provided by filter vendors, who search for sites that meet criteria for being classified as either "objectionable" or "family-friendly."

Filtering software vendors vary greatly in the amount of information and control they make available to users. Most vendors do not allow users to see the actual list of blocked sites, as it is considered to be a kind of trade secret. However, some vendors provide detailed descriptions of the criteria used to determine which sites should be blocked. Some vendors might allow users to add sites to the list, either in their own software or by sending sites to the vendor for review.

Stand-alone filtering tools also vary in the extent to which they can be configured by users. Some software packages allow users to make selections from a list of the categories they would like blocked. For example, a parent may wish to block explicit sex but not discussions of homosexuality as a life-style. Others might allow users to choose from a range of choices in any given topic area. For example, instead of simply blocking all nudity, these tools might allow users to chose to allow partial nudity while blocking full nudity.

Keyword-based blocking uses text searches to categorize sites. If a site contains objectionable words or phrases, it will be blocked.

2.4) What's wrong with list-based filtering?

There are several problems with filtering based on lists of sites to be blocked.

First, these lists are incomplete. Due to the decentralized nature of the Internet, it's practically impossible to definitively search all Internet sites for "objectionable" material. Even with a paid staff searching for sites to block, software vendors cannot hope to identify all sites that meet their blocking criteria. Furthermore, since new web sites are constantly appearing, even regular updates from the software vendor will not block out all adult web sites. Each updated list will be obsolete as soon as it is released, as any as any site that appears after the update will not be on the list, and will not be blocked. The volatility of individual sites is yet another potential cause of trouble. Adult material might be added to (or removed from) a site soon after the site is added to (or removed from) a list of blocked sites.

Blocking lists also raise problems by withholding information from users, who may or may not have access to information describing the criteria used to block web sites. While some vendors provide descriptions of their blocking criteria, this information is often vague or incomplete. Several vendors have extended blocking beyond merely "objectionable" materials. In some instances, political sites and sites that criticize blocking software have been blocked.

This obscurity is compounded by practices used to protect these lists of blocked sites. Vendors often consider these lists to be proprietary intellectual property, which they protect through mathematical encryption, which renders the lists incomprehensible to end users. As a result, users are unable to examine which sites are blocked and why. This arbitrary behavior demeans the user's role as an active, thoughtful participant in their use of the Internet.

2.5) What's wrong with filtering based on keyword searches?

Keyword searching is a crude and inflexible approach that is likely to block sites that should not be blocked while letting "adult" sites pass through unblocked. These problems are tied to two shortcomings of this approach:

Keyword searches cannot use contextual information. While searches can identify the presence of certain words in a text, they cannot evaluate the context in which those words are used. For example, a search might find the word "breast" on a web page, but it cannot determine whether that word was used in a chicken recipe, an erotic story, or in some other manner. In one notable incident, America Online's keyword searches blocked a breast cancer support group.

Keyword searches cannot interpret graphics. It is not currently possible to "search" the contents of a picture. Therefore, a page containing sexually explicit pictures will be blocked only if the text on that page contains one or more words from the list of words to be blocked.

3.0) The Platform for Internet Content Selection (PICS)

3.1) What is PICS?

The Platform for Internet Content Selection (PICS) was developed by the W3 Consortium - the guiding force behind the World-Wide-Web - as a protocol for the exchange of rating information. Paul Resnick - University of Michigan professor and the creator of PICS - described PICS in a Scientific American (March 1997) article:

The Massachusetts Institute of Technology's World Wide Web Consortium has developed a set of technical standards called PICS (Platform for Internet Content Selection) so that people can electronically distribute descriptions of digital works in a simple, computer-readable form. Computers can process these labels in the background, automatically shielding users from undesirable material or directing their attention to sites of particular interest. The original impetus for PICS was to allow parents and teachers to screen materials they felt were inappropriate for children using the Net. Rather than censoring what is distributed, as the Communications Decency Act and other legislative initiatives have tried to do, PICS enables users to control what they receive.

There are two components involved in the practical use of PICS: ratings systems, and software that uses ratings systems to filter content.

3.2) How does PICS-based filtering differ from stand-alone systems?

Stand-alone filtering products generally include lists of sites to be filtered and explicit filtering criteria. Purchasers of these products are tied to the filtering decisions made by the software vendor.

PICS-based software uses an alternative approach based on distributed sharing of ratings information. Instead of using blocking lists or keyword searches, programs that use PICS use standardized "ratings systems" to determine which sites should be blocked. Available from software vendors or from Internet sites, these ratings systems are be used to describe the content of Internet sites (see question 3.7 for a description of how PICS works in practice). Users of PICS-based software are usually given the ability to choose which ratings system they would like to use.

As an open standard, PICS can be used for a wide range of applications. In addition to providing a means for blocking content deemed unsuitable for children, PICS might also be used for describing content in terms of its educational content, potential for violations of privacy, or any other criteria that involve rating of Internet sites.

In some senses, programs that use PICS are much more flexible than stand-alone filtering software. Users of PICS software are not tied to the judgments of the software vendor, and the descriptions of the criteria used by the ratings systems are publicly available. However, users are currently limited to choosing between a small number of ratings systems, each of which has its own biases and viewpoints. Users that disagree with the popular ratings systems may be unable to use PICS in a manner that fits their needs and viewpoints.

3.3) What is a ratings system?

A ratings system is a series of categories and gradations within those categories that can be used to classify content. The categories that are used are chosen by the developer of the ratings system, and may include topics such as such as "sexual content," "race," or "privacy." Each of these categories would be described along different levels of content, such as "Romance; no sex", "Explicit sexual activity," or somewhere in between. Prominent ratings systems currently in use include RSACi, SafeSurf, and NetShepherd.

A rating is a description of some particular Internet content, using the terms and vocabulary of some ratings system.

3.4) How are ratings systems developed?

The PICS developers and the W3 Consortium built PICS to be an open standard, so anyone can create a ratings system. Individuals and groups can develop ratings systems by defining categories and describing ratings within those categories. Once a ratings system is developed, it must be publicized to users and publishers.

3.5) Who rates sites?

The PICS standard describes two approaches to the rating of sites:

Self-Rating: Web site publishers can evaluate their own content and put PICS rating information directly into their web pages. Currently, this evaluation can be done through Web pages provided by developers of the major ratings services.

Third-Party Ratings: Interested third parties can use PICS ratings systems to evaluate web sites and publish their own ratings for these sites. Educational groups, religious groups, or individuals can rate sites and publish these ratings on the Internet for users to access.

3.6) What PICS-based ratings systems can I use?

From a technical perspective, you can use any PICS-based ratings system. However, your practical options are somewhat more limited. While you might configure your browser to use "Joe's Internet Ratings," it's unlikely that many sites have ratings for Joe's system, so it wouldn't be of very much use.

Your browser software may influence choice of ratings service. If you use Microsoft's Internet Explorer, you only have one choice (RSACi) built in to the initial distribution. To use other ratings services, IE users must download files from the Net and install them on their PCs.

Currently (as of September 1997), there are three PICS services that are being widely used or promoted:

RSACi: Sponsored by the Recreational Software Advisory Council (known for ratings on video games), RSACi is probably the most widely used PICS ratings system in use today. RSACi's ratings categories include violence, nudity, sex, and language, with 5 ratings within each category. As of September 1997, RSACi claims to have over 43,000 sites rated.

SafeSurf: Developed by the SafeSurf corporation, this system's categories include "Age Range," "Profanity," "Heterosexual Themes," "Homosexual Themes," "Nudity," "Violence," "Sex, Violence, and Profanity," "Intolerance," "Glorifying Drug Use," "Other Adult Themes," and "Gambling," with 9 distinctions for each category.

SafeSurf and RSACi both rely on self-rating of Internet sites by web publishers.

NetShepherd: Based in Calgary, Net Shepherd rates sites based on quality levels (1-5 stars). Unlike SafeSurf and RSAC, NetShepherd conducts third-party ratings of web sites. They claim to have rated over 300,000 sites. NetShepherd has also announced partnerships with firms such as Altavista and Catholic Telecom, Inc.

3.7) How do I use PICS?

To use PICS, users start by configuring their browsers or PICS software to use a ratings system (such as RSACi or SafeSurf). Once the ratings system is chosen, users must examine each of the categories in order to choose a preferred level of information for that category. In practical terms, this means deciding how much they are willing to allow. For example, one ratings system's choices for nudity include "none," "revealing attire," "partial nudity," "frontal nudity," and "explicit."

Once these choices have been made, the browser software uses them to filter sites. When an Internet site is requested, the browser compares the site's rating with the user's selection. If the site has ratings for the chosen system and those ratings fit within the parameters chosen by the user, it is displayed as usual. If the appropriate ratings fall outside of those parameters (perhaps the site has "frontal nudity," while the user was only willing to accept "partial nudity"), access to the site is prohibited, and the user is shown a message indicating that the site is blocked.

Since most web sites are not currently rated, most software provides users with the option of blocking out sites that do not contain PICS ratings.

In order to prevent mischievous children from changing ratings or disabling PICS altogether, most browsers can be configured to require a password before disabling PICS.

3.8) Should I rate my site?

The answer to this question will depend upon who's being asked.

RSACi, SafeSurf, and other proponents of ratings would obviously like everyone to rate their sites, while civil libertarians and opponents of ratings argue against any ratings.

Publishers of family-oriented sites or those who are trying to reach audiences concerned with Internet content might consider rating. Similarly, purveyors of adult material might rate their sites in order to be "good citizens."

3.9) What should a publisher consider before self-rating?

Web site publishers must decide which (if any) ratings systems to use. Since each ratings system requires a separate valuation process, and separate modifications to web pages, it may not be practical for web-site publishers to use all of the popularly available ratings.

In evaluating ratings systems, publishers may want to examine the categories used by each system and the distinctions used by those categories. Different systems will classify ratings systems in different ways, some of which may misrepresent the content of web sites. For example, sites discussing safe sex might not want to be placed in the same category with pornographic sites.

Web site publishers might also consider the popularity of the ratings services. Currently (as of September 1997), there are only a few major ratings services. Publishers are free to user other ratings, but these may not be useful to the Internet users who rely upon the popular systems. This presents a dilemma for some publishers, who can either accept the ratings of the popular systems, even if those ratings misrepresent their material, or refuse to rate their sites, knowing that this might cause their sites to be unavailable to some users.

Versions of Microsoft's Internet Explorer have provided an extreme example of this problem. Although IE allows user to use any PICS ratings system, RSACi is the only system that is built in to the selection list. Since Internet Explorer is the most widely-used PICS-capable browser (as of fall 1997, Netscape's Navigator does not support PICS), it seems likely that many PICS users will be relying upon RSACi. For publishers interested in reaching a wide audience, this market force may determine their choice of ratings system.

Finally, philosophical concerns may cause some people to decide not to rate. Web-site publishers who are not comfortable with the general content of available ratings systems, or who object to the concept of ratings, may choose not to rate their own sites.

MSNBC's troubles with ratings provide an ironic illustration of this possibility. Displeased with the RSACi ratings that would be necessary, MSNBC management removed all rating information from the site. MSNBC and other news organizations briefly discussed the possibility of creating a new ratings system specifically for news reporting.

While this proposal was eventually rejected, it illustrates some of the problems with content ratings. Well-funded publishers like MSNBC might be able to effectively create ratings systems that meet their needs, but smaller publishers who want to rate their sites may be forced to accept unsatisfactory ratings.

3.10) What concerns are raised by third-party ratings?

Since third-party ratings aren't validated by any technical means, third-party ratings can be easily misused. Just as stand-alone filtering software can block sites for political or business reasons (even if those sites do not contain adult content), third party raters might apply inaccurate labels to web sites in order to make sure that they would be blocked by PICS-compliant software.

To make matters worse, third party rating does not require the consent or even notification of a web-site publisher. Since third party ratings are distributed by third party "label bureaus," a web-site publisher may not know if her pages have been rated, or what the ratings said.

Third-party ratings also present significant technical challenges that may discourage their development. Unlike self-ratings, third party PICS ratings do not reside on publisher's web pages. Instead, they must be distributed to users using one of two methods:

File Transfer: Users could download ratings from the web sites provided by third-party services. For ratings services that cover any significant portion of the Internet, this could easily amount to megabytes of data, which could be cumbersome to download using slow modems. Furthermore, these lists would quickly become obsolete, and would therefore require regular updates. Label Bureaus: Third-party raters (or others) might establish servers that would provide ratings information. In this model, users of a rating service would retrieve a rating from the rating service, and this rating would be used to determine whether or not the site should be blocked. For a widely-used ratings system, this would require computing power and Internet bandwidth capable of handling constant streams of requests for ratings. This might be cost-prohibitive for many potential ratings services.

3.11) What about sites that aren't rated? What if someone puts the wrong rating on a site?

PICS ratings can be truly useful for parents only if a significant percentage of the Internet's web sites are accurately rated. Currently, this is not the case. The

40,000 sites that have self-rated with RSACi, or even the 300,000 sites rated by NetShepherd, represent a small fraction of the total number of web sites available.

Some software, such as Microsoft's Internet Explorer, provides users with the option of blocking out any site that does not have a rating. This choice may be appropriate for some, but it severely restricts the available options. By blocking out most of the Web (including possibly some sites designed for younger users), this approach presents children with a severely restricted view of the world.

The accuracy of PICS ratings is obviously a concern. For example, unscrupulous purveyors of adult material might attempt to use an inaccurate rating in an attempt to slip through PICS filters. In RSACi's terms of use, the RSAC reserves the right to audit sites in order to guarantee accuracy of ratings. SafeSurf takes this one step further. The proposed Online Cooperative Publishing Act calls for legal penalties for sites that label inaccurately, or refuse to rate. In June 1997, Sen. Patty Murray (D-Washington) proposed the Child-safe Internet Act of 1997, which called for similar penalties. While these legislative suggestions might be effective in promoting the use of ratings, they raise serious concerns in terms of first-amendment rights and possibilities for overly aggressive enforcement. Question 4.1 discusses these possibilities in more depth. There are currently no quality controls on third-party ratings.

These issues of quality and accountability would become even trickier if numerous schemes were to come into use. If there were dozens of PICS ratings schemes to choose from, publishers would not know which to choose, and users might not know which to trust.

3.12) What if I don't like the ratings systems that are available? Can individuals and organizations start new ratings systems?

Currently, there are two choices for individuals and organizations that are uncomfortable with the existing ratings systems.

The first - and currently the only viable alternative - is to avoid use of PICS for self-rating, and in Internet browsers.

The second approach would be to develop a new ratings vocabulary, as an alternative to RSACi, SafeSurf, or other currently available ratings systems. This involves several steps:

The first step is generation of a ratings system, including categories that would be discussed and distinctions within those categories. This would require a discussion of the values that will be represented in the ratings system, and how these values should be expressed.

Once the system has been developed, sites must be rated. This can be done in one of two ways:

The developers of the ratings system could convince web-site publishers to self-rate. This would require significant resources, as raising awareness of the new ratings system through advertising, press contacts, and other means can be quite expensive. Of course, this new ratings system would raise "chicken-and-the-egg" concerns. Why should publishers use this system for self-rating unless they know that it's being used? And, conversely, why should users choose a ratings system that doesn't have very many sites rated? The new ratings system can create third-party ratings for the Web. This would also require significant human resources to generate these ratings. If we assume that workers could generate these ratings at a rate of 1/minute, or 480 over the course of an 8-hour day, it would take 8 people working 40-hour weeks roughly an entire year to rate one million web sites. Of course, the Internet already has more than one million sites, and it will have grown significantly before those 8 people finish their year of ratings work. Furthermore, workers rating web sites at this rate would probably make more than a few mistakes in their choice of ratings. As described in question 3.10, distribution of third-party ratings also presents significant technical challenges and expenses.

Once the ratings have been generated for the web sites, the new ratings system must be publicized to potential users. As described above, this could be expensive and difficult.

Given the significant resources that will be needed to effectively deploy a new ratings system, it seems unlikely that there will be a large number of PICS alternatives available in the near future. The developers of PICS are trying to change this through the PICS Incubator project, which offers resources to organizations interested in developing new ratings systems.

3.13) What's wrong with PICS and Internet ratings in general?

In theory, there are many useful applications of rating information.

Book reviews and movie ratings are only two examples of the many ways in which we use information filters. Used in conjunction with other information sources - including advertising and word-of-mouth - these ratings provide a basis for making informed decisions regarding information.

Unfortunately, PICS does not currently provide users with the contextual information and range of choices necessary for informed decision making. When deciding which movies to see, we have access to reviews, advertisements and trailers which provide information regarding the content. These details help us choose intelligently based on our values and preferences. On the other hand, PICS-based systems do not provide any contextual detail: users are simply told that access to a site is denied because the site's rating exceeds a certain value on the rating scale.

Furthermore, the limited range of currently available PICS ratings system does not provide users with a meaningful choice between alternatives. Parents who are not comfortable with any of the current ratings systems may not find PICS to be a viable alternative.

Continuing with our analogies to other media, consider book reviews in a world where only two or three publications reviewed books. This might work very well for people who agree with the opinions of these reviewers (and, of course, for the reviewers themselves!), but it would work very poorly for those who have differing viewpoints.

Some might argue that the "success" of a single set of movie ratings offers a model for PICS. However, ratings are generally applied only to movies made for entertainment by major producers. Documentaries and educational films are generally not rated, but similar web sites could be rated under PICS.

Movie ratings also provide a cautionary lesson that should be considered with respect to the Internet. Unrated movies, or movies with certain ratings, often have a difficult time reaching audiences, as they may not be shown in certain theaters or carried by large video chains. This has led to self-censorship, as directors trim explicit scenes in order to avoid NC-17 ratings. This may be appropriate for commercially-oriented entertainment, but it could be dangerous when applied to safe-sex information on the Internet.

Ratings systems also fail to account for the global nature of the Internet. Legal or practical pressures aimed at convincing Internet publishers to rate their own sites will have little effect, as these businesses or individuals have the option of simply moving their material to a foreign country. Furthermore, the existing ratings systems are of limited value to those in countries that do not share western values.

Concerns about unrated international material or differing cultural values could be addressed through direct censorship. For example, governments might use PICS ratings or proprietary filtering software to implement "national firewalls" which would screen out objectionable material. Alternatively, ratings might be used to "punish" inappropriate speech. If search engines chose to block sites with certain ratings (or unrated sites), or if browsers blocked certain ratings (or lack of ratings) by default, these sites might never be seen.

It is possible that a wide range of PICS ratings system could come into use, providing families with a real opportunity to choose ratings that meet their values. The utility of PICS might also be increased by use of new technologies like "metadata" (data about data, used to describe the content of web pages and other information resources), which might be used to provide contextual information along with PICS ratings. However, these tools may not be available for general use for some time, if at all.

Some people confuse ratings with the topical organization that is used in libraries and Web sites like Yahoo. While no system of organization of information is neutral, topical schemes attempt to describe what a resource is "about." Rating rarely helps us find information resources topically and is usually too narrowly focused on a few criteria to be useful for information retrieval.

4.0) Alternatives

4.1) Can anything work?

The answer to this question will depend largely on the perspective of the asker.

If this question is taken to mean: "Are there any solutions that would provide children with the ability to use the Internet without ever seeing material that is explicit or 'adult,'" the answer is probably yes. This would require a combination of three factors:

> 1. Legislation requiring "accurate" ratings and specifying penalties for those who do not comply.

2.Technical measures to prevent the transmission of unlabeled material, or any material from foreign sites (which would not be subject to US laws).

3.Mandatory use of filtering software, using mandated settings.

The obvious legal, political, and practical problems with this scenario would certainly doom it to failure. While mandated standards have been suggested by some groups, it is quite likely that they would be found unconstitutional and in violation of the Supreme Court's *Reno v. ACLU* decision that overturned key provisions of the Communications Decency Act. Furthermore, the accuracy of content ratings is a matter of judgment that would not easily be legislated. Practically, laws requiring the use of filtering software would be virtually unenforceable. Finally, if efforts aimed at "sanitizing" the Internet somehow managed to survive legal challenges, they would have a chilling effect upon speech on the Internet.

If the question is interpreted as meaning: "Are there any solutions that provide some protection from adult or objectionable material without restricting free speech?" the answer is much less clear. Stand-alone systems clearly don't meet these criteria, as they place users at the whims of software vendors, who may block sites for arbitrary reasons. In theory, PICS might fit this role, but the lack of a meaningful choice between substantially different ratings systems leaves parents and publishers with the choice of using ratings that they may not agree with, or that fail to adequately describe their needs or materials.

Describing speech as "adult" or "appropriate for children" is inherently a tricky and value-laden process. In the U.S., many people have attempted to prevent schools and libraries from using everyday publications like Huckleberry Finn and descriptions of gay/lesbian lifestyles. The fierce debates over these efforts show that no consensus can be reached. Increased use of filtering software would likely be the beginning, rather than the end, of debates regarding what Internet materials are "appropriate" for children, and who gets to make that decision.

4.2) I understand that there are many problems with filters and ratings. What can I do to protect my children?

The first thing that parents should do is to consider the extent of the problem. While some news reports might leave parents with the impression that the Internet is nothing but pornography, this is far from the case. In fact, it's unlikely that children would randomly stumble across pornographic material. Furthermore, many adult sites have explicit warnings or require payment by credit card, which further decrease the chances of children "accidentally" finding pornography.

Secondly, parents should play an active role and interest in their children's use of the Internet. For some children this might mean restricting Internet use to closely supervised sessions. Other children might be able to work with clearly defined rules and guidelines. To discourage unsupervised use of the Internet, parents might consider measures such as placing the family computer in a common space in the home and retaining adult control over any passwords required for Internet access.

Parents should also work to educate children regarding proper use of the Internet. Just as parents teach children not to talk to strangers on the street, parents might discourage children from visiting certain web sites, divulging personal or family information, or participating in inappropriate chats.

Some parents might consider using filtering software, despite all of the potential drawbacks. Parents considering this route should closely examine their options, in order to understand their options and the implications of any choice.

For stand-alone filtering systems, this means investigating the criteria used in developing blocking lists and/or news reports describing the software. If possible, parents might try to find stand-alone systems that allow users to view and edit the lists of blocked sites.

Parents considering the use of PICS systems should investigate the categories used by the various ratings systems, in order to find one that meets their needs. Information about PICS-based systems can be found at the home pages of the respective ratings systems.

In general, the use of a filtering product involves an implicit acceptance of the criteria used to generate the ratings involved. Before making this decision, parents should take care to insure that the values behind the ratings are compatible with their beliefs.

Finally, parents should realize that the Internet is just a reflection of society in general. Much of the "adult" content on the Internet can be found on cable TV, at local video stores, or in movie theaters. Since other media fail to shield children from violence or sexual content, restrictions on the Internet will always be incomplete.

4.3) What roles can ISPs play?

Some have called upon ISPs to play a greater role in helping parents filter the Net for their children. There are two ways that ISPs might participate in these efforts:

ISP-Based Filtering: ISPs might do the filtering themselves, preventing their customers from accessing objectionable materials, even if those customers do not have their own filtering software. This requires the use of a proxy server, which would serve as a broker between the ISP's customers and remote web sites. When a customer of a filtering ISP wants to see a web site, his request goes to the proxy server operated by the ISP. The proxy server will then check to see if the site should be blocked. If the site is allowable, the proxy server retrieves the web page and returns it to the customer.

This approach is technically feasible. In fact, it's currently used by many corporations, and some ISPs that offer this service. However, proxying requires significant computational resources that may be beyond the means of smaller ISPs. Even if the ISP can afford the computers and Internet bandwidth needed, this approach is still far from ideal. In order to do the filtering, proxy servers would have to use stand-alone or PICS-based systems, so they would be subject to the limitations of these technologies (see 2.4, 2.5, and 3.13). The shortcomings of existing filtering systems may prove particularly troublesome for ISPs that advertise filtering services, as these firms could be embarrassed or worse if their filters fail to block adult material. Finally, ISPs that filter material may lose customers who are interested in unfiltered access to the Internet.

Providing Filtering Software: Others have suggested that ISPs should be required to provide users with filtering software. While this might be welcome by parents who are thinking about getting on to the Net (and by software vendors!) it could present a financial serious burden for smaller ISPs.

4.4) What about Internet access in libraries?

Internet access in public libraries has been a contentious area of discussion. Claiming concern for children using library computers to access the Internet, numerous municipalities have installed, or are considering installing filtering software on publicly-accessible Internet terminals. However, as cyberspace lawyer, publisher, and free-speech activist Jonathan Wallace has pointed out, the use of blocking software in public libraries may be unconstitutional:

Most advocates of the use of blocking software by libraries have forgotten that the public library is a branch of government, and therefore subject to First Amendment rules which prohibit content-based censorship of speech. These rules apply to the acquisition or the removal of Internet content by a library. Secondly, government rules classifying speech by the acceptability of content (in libraries or elsewhere) are inherently suspect, may not be vague or overbroad, and must conform to existing legal parameters laid out by the Supreme Court. Third, a library may not delegate to a private organization, such as the publisher of blocking software, the discretion to determine what library users may see. Fourth, forcing patrons to ask a librarian to turn off blocking software has a chilling effect under the First Amendment.

5.0) Where Can I Find More Information?

World-Wide-Web Consortium PICS Home Page: http://www.w3.org/PICS

The PICS Incubator Project: http://www.si.umich.edu/~presnick/PICS-incubatorIncubator Project

RSACi: http://www.rsac.org

SafeSurf: http://www.safesurf.com

NetShepherd: http://www.netshepherd.com

CyberPatrol: http://www.cyberpatrol.com

NetNanny: http://www.netnanny.com

Fahrenheit 451.2: Is Cyberspace Burning - The ACLU's Report on Filtering Software: http://www.aclu.org/issues/cyber/burning.html

Peacefire: http://www.peacefire.org

The Censorware Project: http://www.spectacle.org/cwp/

The Global Internet Liberty Campaign: http://www.gilc.org/speech/ratings

The Internet Free Expression Alliance: http://www.ifea.net

Families Against Internet Censorship: http://home.rmi.net/~fagin/faic

Computer Professionals for Social Responsibility (CPSR): http://www.cpsr.org

6) Credits

6.1) Who gets the credit?

This document grew out of discussions held by CPSR's Cyber-Rights working group and other concerned individuals during the summer of 1997. Andy Oram, Craig Johnson, Karen Coyle, Marcy Gordon, Bennett Hasleton, Jean-Michel Andre, and Aki Namioka provided invaluable assistance. Please feel free to distribute or copy this document. Comments can be sent to hhochheiser@cpsr.org.

6.2) Who is CPSR?

CPSR is a public-interest alliance of computer scientists and others concerned about the impact of computer technology on society. We work to influence decisions regarding the development and use of computers because those decisions have far-reaching consequences and reflect our basic values and priorities. As technical experts, CPSR members provide the public and policymakers with realistic assessments of the power, promise, and limitations of computer technology. As concerned citizens, we direct public attention to critical choices concerning the applications of computing and how those choices affect society.

Submission to the World Wide Web Consortium on PICSRules

Global Internet Liberty Campaign

December 1997

We, the undersigned members of the Global Internet Liberty Campaign (GILC), make the following submission in relation to the W3C Proposed Recommendation "PICSRules 1.1" dated 4 November 1997 (http://www.w3.org/TR/PR-PICSRules.htm).

GILC members are concerned with matters of human rights, civil liberty, and personal freedom.

Noting that:

- Article 19 of the Universal Declaration of Human Rights explicitly protects freedom of expression for all and specifically the "freedom to hold opinions without interference and to seek, receive and impart information and ideas through any media".

- This principle has been reaffirmed in multiple international agreements, including the International Covenant on Civil and Political Rights.

- W3C's mission is "to realize the full potential of the Web: as an elegant machine-to-machine system, as a compelling human-to-computer interface, and as an efficient human-human communications medium".

- PICSRules 1.1 have been developed for, or can be used for, the purposes of:

    - preventing individuals from using the Internet to exchange information on topics that may be controversial or unpopular,

- enabling the development of country profiles to facilitate a global/universal rating system desired by governments,

- blocking access to content on entire domains, via the specification of full or partial domain names and/or IP addresses, regardless of the username, port number, or particular file path that is specified in the URL,

- blocking access to Internet content available at any domain or page which contains a specific key-word or character string in the URL,

- over-riding self-rating labels provided by content creators and providers.

- PICSRules 1.1 go far beyond the original objective of PICS to empower Internet users to control what they and those under their care access. They further facilitate the implementation of server/ proxy-based filtering thus providing a more simplified means of enabling upstream censorship, beyond the control of the end user.

We draw to W3C's attention that:

- similar techniques that block Internet sites have prevented access to innocuous speech, either by deliberate intent, through oversight, or as a result of ignorance of the infrastructure of the Web,

- repressive governments are desirous of a more easily implementable, technological, means of restricting information their citizens are able to access and inhibiting their communications with others,

- methods to restrict the ability of citizens to gain access to information and to communicate with others are contrary to principles of free expression and democratic society,

- PICSRules 1.1, in enabling the use of wildcards in IP addresses, etc, facilitate blocking of not only entire domains, but of the majority of content originating from specified countries,

- the rapidly increasing number of people accessing the Web discredits the perception, of various government and industry representatives, that limitations on content accessibility are essential to provide a climate of confidence for the furtherance of electronic commerce. In fact, filtering and rating systems intended for the protection of minors have proven inefficient and counter-productive,

- the ability of community organisations to develop a ratings system applicable to their values, a stated original intent of PICS, is not enhanced by the complex, albeit sophisticated, language of PICSRules 1.1.

Whilst the W3C media release of 25 November 1997 states that:

> "PICSRules is a mechanism for exchanging user settings, resulting in an easy one-click configuration...With PICSRules parents can go to a PTA site and download initial settings which are recommended for primary school children ..."

even a cursory analysis of PICSRules 1.1 indicates that the likelihood of community organisations developing complex profiles is slim. The necessary expertise is more likely to be acquired by governments seeking to restrict access to content and inhibit freedom of expression.

PICSRules 1.1 are clearly intended to serve the purpose of enabling the empowered to restrict the ability of the unempowered to communicate.

It seems apparent that PICSRules have been developed in response to calls from governments who seek a more efficient and effective technological means of restricting human-to-human communications. European and Australian governments, at the least, are involved in the development of a global rating system which will be enabled by PICSRules 1.1. Mandatory labelling of content has already been proposed in the UK, Australia, USA. The ability of governments to restrict access and freedom of expression through the use of firewalls /proxies will be enhanced by the adoption of PICSRules 1.1.

In view of the above, we oppose the proposed adoption of PICSRules 1.1 on the grounds that they will provide a tool for widespread global censorship, which will conflict with W3C's mission to "realize the full potential of the Web...as an efficient human-human communications medium".

We call on W3C to reject the proposals of the PICSRules Working Group and direct resources towards working on genuine metadata systems which will facilitate easier and faster access to desired classes of information by all Internet users, rather than solely supporting denial of access.

Background:

American Civil Liberties Union (ACLU) (USA): "Fahrenheit 451.2: Is Cyberspace Burning? – How Rating and Blocking Proposals May Torch Free Speech on the Internet" (http://www.aclu.org/issues/cyber/burning.html)

Computer Professionals for Social Responsibility (CPSR) (USA): "Filtering FAQ" (http://quark.cpsr.org/~harryh/faq.html)

Cyber-Rights & Cyber-Liberties (UK): "Who Watches the Watchmen: Internet Content Rating Systems, and Privatised Censorship" (http://www.leeds.ac.uk/law/pgs/yaman/watchmen.htm)

Electronic Privacy Information Center (USA): "Faulty Filters: How Content Filters Block Access to Kid-Friendly Information on the Internet" (http://www2.epic.org/reports/filter-report.html)

Imaginons un Reseau Internet Solidaire (IRIS) (F): "Labeling and Filtering: Possibilities, Dangers, and Perspectives" (http://girafe.ensba.fr/iris/rapport-ce/annexe6.html)

This submission is made by the following organisations:

Associazione per la Libertà nella Comunicazione Elettronica Interattiva (ALCEI)
http://www.nexus.it/alcei.html

American Civil Liberties Union
http://www.aclu.org/

Bulgarian Institute for Legal Development
http://www.bild.acad.bg/

CommUnity - The Computer Communicators Association
http://www.community.org.uk/

Computer Professionals for Social Responsibility
http://www.cpsr.org/home.html

Cyber-Rights & Cyber-Liberties (UK)
http://www.leeds.ac.uk/law/pgs/yaman/yaman.htm

Derechos Human Rights
http://www.derechos.org/

Electronic Frontiers Australia
http://www.efa.org.au/

Electronic Frontier Foundation
http://www.eff.org

Electronic Privacy Information Center
http://www.epic.org/

FITUG e.V. Foerderkreis Informationstechnik
und Gesellschaft
http://www.fitug.de/

Fronteras Electrónicas España (FrEE)
http://www.arnal.es/free

Human Rights Watch
http://www.hrw.org/

Imaginons un Reseau Internet Solidaire
http://girafe.ensba.fr/iris/

NetAction
http://www.netaction.org/

Peacefire
http://www.peacefire.org/

Privacy International
http://www.privacy.org/pi/

quintessenz
http://www.quintessenz.at/entrance/index.html

Impact of Self-Regulation and Filtering on Human Rights to Freedom of Expression

Global Internet Liberty Campaign

Presented to OECD "Internet Content Self-Regulation Dialogue,"

March 25, 1998, Paris.

Principles

The Global Internet Liberty Campaign is a group of human rights and civil liberties organisations which advocate the following:

- Prohibiting prior censorship of on-line communication.

- Requiring that laws restricting the content of online speech distinguish between the liability of content providers and the liability of data carriers.

- Insisting that on-line free expression not be restricted by indirect means such as excessively restrictive governmental or private controls over computer hardware or software, telecommunications infrastructure, or other essential components of the Internet.

- Including citizens in the Global Information Infrastructure (Internet) development process from countries that are currently unstable economically, have insufficient infrastructure, or lack sophisticated technology.

- Prohibiting discrimination on the basis of race, colour, sex, language, religion, political or other opinion, national or social origin, property, birth or other status.

- Ensuring that personal information generated on the Internet for one purpose is not used for an unrelated purpose or disclosed without the person's informed consent and enabling individuals to review personal information on the Internet and to correct inaccurate information.

- Allowing on-line users to encrypt their communications and information without restriction.

We, the undersigned members of the Global Internet Liberty Campaign consider that the following issues are important with respect to Content and Conduct on the Internet.

Human Rights Doctrines Protecting Freedom of Expression are Fully Applicable to the Internet

International human rights law enshrines the rights to freedom of expression and access to information. These core documents explicitly protect freedom of expression "without regard to borders," a phrase especially pertinent to the global Internet:

> "Everyone has the right to freedom of opinion and expression; this right includes freedom to hold opinions without interference and to seek, receive and impart information and ideas through any media, and regardless of frontiers." (Article 19, Universal Declaration of Human Rights).

> "Everyone shall have the right to freedom of expression; this right shall include freedom to seek, receive, and impart information and ideas of all kinds, regardless of frontiers, either orally, in writing or in print, in the form of art, or through any other media of his choice." (Article 19, International Covenant on Civil and Political Rights).

> "Everyone has the right to freedom of expression. This right shall include freedom to hold opinions and to receive and impart information and ideas without interference by public authority and regardless of borders." (Article 10, European Convention for the Protection of Human Rights and Fundamental Freedoms).

Freedom of Speech is Fundamental on the Internet

The Internet is a unique communication medium and is more than a meer industry. Like no other medium before, it allows individuals to express their ideas and opinions directly to a world audience, while allowing them access to other ideas, opinions and information to which they may not otherwise have access.

While the mass media usually responds to the economic and political interests of those who control it, such controls do not presently exist on the Internet. Here, citizens from the most repressive regimes are able to find information about matters concerning their governments or their human rights records that no local newspaper may dare print, while denouncing the conditions under which they live, for the world to hear. The Internet allows us an intimate look at other countries, other people and other cultures which few before were ever able to attain. This power to give and receive information, so central to any conception of democracy, can be truly achieved on the Internet, as nowhere before.

This unprecedented power, however, can be very threatening to repressive regimes. Traditional methods of censorship – embargoing newspapers, threatening journalists, closing down presses – do not work on the Internet – the censoring techniques that these regimes will engage in, and their rationalisations, are not as well unknown, but they can be just as destructive.

Free Expression on the Internet Enhances Democracy, Culture, and the Economy

- The vast majority of Internet use is for legitimate purposes;

- The effect of access and use of this global interactive medium has been to promote and defend civil and political rights worldwide;

- The experiences of communities in different countries indicates that few things could be more threatening to authoritarian regimes than access and use of the medium which knows no boundaries and is very hard to control;

- On the Internet, citizens are not mere consumers of content but also creators of content and the content on the Internet is as diverse as human thought. (from the judgment against the US Communications Decency Act); and

- Individuals and communities have been using the new-found freedom online to link, interact and work collectively in this global work space. This fundamental shift in power has created a possibility for every individual to be a publisher.

Anonymity

Central to free expression and the protection of privacy is the right to express political beliefs without fear of retribution and to control the disclosure of personal identity. Protecting the right of anonymity is therefore an essential goal for the protection of personal freedoms in the online world.

The right of anonymity is recognized in law and accepted by custom. It has been an integral part of the growth and development of the Internet. Some governments are working to extend techniques for anonymity. The Netherlands and the Canadian provence of Ontario are pursuing a study on anonymity. The German government has recently adopted legislation that would encourage the adoption of anonymous payments systems for the Internet.

But other efforts are underway to establish mandatory identification requirements and to limit the use of techniques that protect anonymity. For example, the G-8 recently considered a proposal to require caller identification for Internet users. Some local governments have also tried to adopt legislation that would prohibit access to the Internet without the disclosure of personal identity.

- Governments should not require the identification of Internet users or restrict the ability to express political beliefs on the Internet anonymously.

- Efforts to develop new techniques to protect anonymity and indentity should be encouraged The governments of Canada, Germany, and the Netherland are to be commended for their recent efforts to suppport anonymity.

- ISPs should not establish unnecessary indentification requirements for customers and should, wherever practicable, preserve the right of users to access the Internet anonymously.

"Self-Regulation," Criminal Law and the Need for Due Process

As with any other sphere of human interaction, criminal activity exists online, as well as offline. The role of an Internet Service Provider is crucial for access to the Internet and because of the crucial role that they play they have been targeted by law enforcement agencies in many countries to act as content censors.

While Internet Service Providers ought to provide law enforcement reasonable assistance in investigating criminal activity, confusing the role of private companies and police authorities risks substantial violation of individual civil liberties.

"Self-regulation" in the Context of the Internet is a Misnomer

In the normal sense of the phrase "self-regulation" is when a group of people, or companies decide that in their own best interest, they should themselves regulate how they go about their joint interests. In the eyes of those who would see the "Internet Industry" "self-regulate", the "industry" must include all content providers, which includes many who's only connection with the Internet is that they use it. What is being suggested in the name of "self-regulation" is not that ISP's should as a group regulate their own behaviour, but that of their customers.

What is often promoted as Internet "self-regulation" is nothing of the sort. Rather it is "privatised censorship". That's not "private", but "privat-ISED," referring to the fairly common occurrence of having a formerly direct government function turned over to administration by a private agency. It's a more sophisticated means of achieving the same goal. The backing is still state power and government threat, but the actual implementation and mechanics of the suppression of material is delegated to a trade group.

"Self-regulatory" regimes ought not to place private ISPs in the role of police officers for the Internet

While we applaud the efforts of ISPs that provide responsible assistance to police in the investigation of crime, it is essential that private entities not take on the role of police or prosecutors.

- Due process: "Self-regulatory" regimes in which a group of ISPs combine to remove possibly illegal material in advance of legal judgement by competent public authorities denies individual speakers due process and risks substantial suppression of protected, though possibly controversial, speech. No matter how careful the guidelines employed by such groups are, the act of removing speech from the Internet on the theory that it might be illegal, without a legal finding to that effect, is an inappropriate suppression of speech. Moreover, if such a self-regulatory regime has the general support of the government, it may even constitute state censorship.

- Incentive for "self-regulators" to over-censor: When ISPs come together to self-regulate certain classes of content in exchange for some limit on legal liability for that content, the overwhelming pressure will be to censor more material, rather than less, in an effort by ISPs to be certain that they have removed any material that might be illegal. Where ISPs are dependent on government grants of liability limitations, their "self-regulating" actions must satisfy the perceived demands of law enforcement, even if this results in removal of legal, protected speech.

- A recent EU communication paper stated that ISPs play a key role in giving users access to Internet content. It should not however be forgotten that the prime responsibility for content lies with authors and content providers. Blocking access at the level of access providers has been criticised by the EU communication paper on the ground that these actions go far beyond the limited category of illegal content and such a restrictive regime is inconceivable for Europe as it would severely interfere with the freedom of the individual and its political traditions.

"Self-regulatory" Regimes have not yet Proven Effective

Initial reports from "self-regulatory" systems cast doubt on their effectiveness and suggest that the only effective way to combat crime such as child pornography is with well trained police. The two most important hotlines in Europe, the Dutch hotline and the UK hotline, have observed that despite the large amount of complaints they receive, this amount is tiny compared to the vast volume available on the Internet. The effects these hotlines have on dissemination of illegal content is also tiny. The Dutch Hotline, in its annual report, warned that it had absolutely no effect on distribution of illegal content in chat-boxes and E-mail, and that its influence on such distribution in newsgroups was very limited. And, according to the Internet Watch Foundation Annual Report, of the 4300 items blocked by private action, "[o]nly the few articles appearing to have originated in the UK are suitable for investigation and action by the UK police." Thus with little measurable law enforcement impact, thousands of presumable legal items were nevertheless removed from the Internet.

Filtering, Rating and Labeling Systems Pose Risks to the Free Flow of Information and Can Be Used by Governments to Violate Human Rights

Blocking, filtering, and labelling techniques can restrict freedom of expression and limit access to information.

Specifically, such techniques can prevent individuals from using the Internet to exchange information on topics that may be controversial or unpopular, enable the development of country profiles to facilitate a global/universal rating system desired by governments, block access to content on entire domains, block access to Internet content available at any domain or page which contains a specific keyword or character string in the URL, and over-ride self-rating labels provided by content creators and providers.

- Government-mandated use of blocking, filtering, and label systems violates basic international human rights protections: No matter what the means, government restriction on speech or access to speech of others violates basic freedom of expression protections.

- Global rating or labeling systems squelch the free flow of information: Efforts to force all Internet speech to be labelled or rated according to a single classification system distorts the fundamental cultural diversity of the Internet and will lead to domination of one set of political or moral viewpoints. Such systems will either be easy to use and not have enough categories for all cultures or it will have so many categories to cater for all cultures that it will be unusable. These systems are antithetical to the Internet and should be rejected.

- Infrastructure distortions to force labeling must be rejected: Extra-legal means of forcing individuals to use filtering, labels or ratings such as ratings requirements in search engines or default settings in browsers restrict the free flow of information online and distort the basic openness of the Internet.

- Transparency must be maintained: Users must be made aware if their Internet access is being filtering, and, if so, based on what filtering system. They must also be able to diable the filtering at any point.

- White lists, rather than black list are preferable: Access to a variety of tools which make positive suggestions (white lists) pointing to certain content, rather than blocking content (black lists), should be encouraged.

- Filtering is inappropriate in public educational institutions and libraries.

- Diversity is essential: To the extent that individuals choses to employ filtering tools, it is vital that they have access to a wide variety of such tools.

List of Signatories

ALCEI - Electronic Frontiers Italy
American Civil Liberties Union
Bulgarian Institute for Legal Development
Center for Democracy and Technology
CITADEL Electronic Frontier France
CommUnity, The Computer Communicators' Association (UK)
Computer Professionals for Social Responsibility
Cyber-Rights & Cyber-Liberties (UK)
Derechos Human Rights
Digital Citizens Foundation Netherlands (DB-NL)
Electronic Frontier Canada
Electronic Frontier Foundation
Electronic Frontiers Australia
Electronic Privacy Information Center
Equipo Nizkor
Fronteras Electronicas Espanya
Index on Censorship
Imaginons un Réseau Internet Solidaire
NetAction
Privacy International
Quintessenz User Group

Mission Statement

Internet Free Expression Alliance

The Internet is a powerful and positive forum for free expression. It is the place where "any person can become a town crier with a voice that resonates farther than it could from any soapbox," as the U.S. Supreme Court recently observed. Internet users, online publishers, library and academic groups and free speech and journalistic organizations share a common interest in opposing the adoption of techniques and standards that could limit the vibrance and openness of the Internet as a communications medium. Indeed, content "filtering" techniques already have been implemented in ways inconsistent with free speech principles, impeding the ability of Internet users to publish and receive constitutionally protected expression.

The Internet Free Expression Alliance will work to:

- Ensure the continuation of the Internet as a forum for open, diverse and unimpeded expression and to maintain the vital role the Internet plays in providing an efficient and democratic means of distributing information around the world;

- Promote openness and encourage informed public debate and discussion of proposals to rate and/or filter online content;

- Identify new threats to free expression and First Amendment values on the Internet, whether legal or technological;

- Oppose any governmental effort to promote, coerce or mandate the rating or filtering of online content;

- Protect the free speech and expression rights of both the speaker and the audience in the interactive online environment;

- Ensure that Internet speakers are able to reach the broadest possible interested audience and that Internet listeners are able to access all material of interest to them;

- Closely examine technical proposals to create filtering architectures and oppose approaches that conceal the filtering criteria employed, or irreparably damage the unique character of the Internet; and

- Encourage approaches that highlight "recommended" Internet content, rather than those that restrict access to materials labelled as "harmful" or otherwise objectionable, and emphasize that any rating that exists solely to allow specific content to be blocked from view may inhibit the flow of free expression.

Member Organizations

American Booksellers Foundation for Free Expression
American Civil Liberties Union
American Society of Newspaper Editors
Association of Independent Video and Filmmakers
Boston Coalition for Freedom of Expression
Computer Professionals for Social Responsibility
Electronic Frontier Foundation
Electronic Privacy Information Center
Feminists for Free Expression
First Amendment Project
Gay & Lesbian Alliance Against Defamation
Human Rights Watch
Institute for Global Communications
International Periodical Distributors Association
Journalism Education Association
National Association of Artists Organizations
National Campaign for Freedom of Expression
National Coalition Against Censorship
National Writers Union
NetAction
Oregon Coalition for Free Expression
Peacefire
PEN American Center
People for the American Way

Publishers Marketing Association
Society of Professional Journalists
The Censorware Project
Washington Independent Writers
z publishing

Censorship in a Box: Why Blocking Software is Wrong for Public Libraries

American Civil Liberties Union

Executive Summary

> The Internet is rapidly becoming an essential tool for learning and communication. But the dream of universal Internet access will remain only a dream if politicians force libraries and other institutions to use blocking software whenever patrons log on.

This special report by the American Civil Liberties Union provides an in depth look at why mandatory blocking software is both inappropriate and unconstitutional in libraries. We do not evaluate any particular product, but rather seek to demonstrate how all blocking software censors valuable speech and gives librarians, educators and parents a false sense of security when providing minors with Internet access.

Our report follows up an August 1997 ACLU special report, "Fahrenheit 451.2: Is Cyberspace Burning?" in which we warned that government coerced, industry efforts to rate content on the Internet could torch free speech online. In that report, we offered a set of guidelines for Internet Service Providers and other industry groups contemplating ratings schemes.

Similarly, in Censorship in a Box, we offer a set of guidelines for libraries and schools looking for alternatives to clumsy and ineffective blocking software:

- Acceptable Use Policies. Schools should develop carefully worded policies that provide instructions for parents, teachers, students, librarians and patrons on use of the Internet.

- Time Limits. Instead of blocking, schools and libraries can establish content-neutral time limits as to when and how young people should use the Internet. Schools can also request that Internet access be limited to school-related work.

- "Driver's Ed" for Internet Users. Students should be taught to engage critical thinking skills when using the Internet and to be careful about relying on inaccurate resources online. One way to teach these skills in schools is to condition Internet access for minors on successful completion of a seminar similar to a driver's education course. Such seminars could also emphasize the dangers of disclosing personally identifiable information and communicating about intimate matters with strangers.

- Recommended Reading. Libraries and schools should publicize and provide links to websites that have been recommended for children and teens.

- Privacy Screens. To avoid unwanted viewing of websites by passers-by – and to protect users' privacy when viewing sensitive information – libraries and schools should place privacy screens around Internet access terminals in a way that minimizes public view

Taken together, these approaches work much better than restrictive software that teaches no critical thinking skills and works only when students are using school or library computers.

Like any technology, blocking software can be used for constructive or destructive purposes. In the hands of parents and others who voluntarily use it, it is a tool that can be somewhat useful in blocking access to some inappropriate material online. But in the hands of government, blocking software is nothing more than censorship in a box.

Introduction

In libraries and schools across the nation, the Internet is rapidly becoming an essential tool for learning and communication. According to the American Library Association, of the nearly 9,000 public libraries in America, 60.4 percent offer Internet access to the public, up from 27.8 percent in 1996. And a recent survey of 1,400 teachers revealed that almost half use the Internet as a teaching tool. But today, unfettered access to the Internet is being threatened by the proliferation of blocking software in libraries.

America's libraries have always been a great equalizer, providing books and other information resources to help people of all ages and backgrounds live, learn, work and govern in a democratic society. Today more than ever, our nation's libraries are vibrant multi-cultural institutions that connect people in the smallest and most remote communities with global information resources.

In 1995, the National Telecommunications and Information Administration of the U.S. Department of Commerce concluded that "public libraries can play a vital role in assuring that advanced information services are universally available to all segments of the American population on an equitable basis. Just as libraries traditionally made available the marvels and imagination of the human mind to all, libraries of the future are planning to allow everyone to participate in the electronic renaissance."

Today, the dream of universal access will remain only a dream if politicians force libraries and other institutions to use blocking software whenever patrons access the Internet. Blocking software prevents users from accessing a wide range of valuable information, including such topics as art, literature, women's health, politics, religion and free speech. Without free and unfettered access to the Internet, this exciting new medium could become, for many Americans, little more than a souped-up, G-rated television network.

This special report by the American Civil Liberties Union provides an in depth look at why mandatory blocking software is both inappropriate and unconstitutional in libraries. We do not offer an opinion about any particular blocking product, but we will demonstrate how all blocking software censors valuable speech and gives librarians, educators and parents a false sense of security when providing minors with Internet access.

Like any technology, blocking software can be used for constructive or destructive purposes. In the hands of parents and others who voluntarily use it, it is a tool that can be somewhat useful in blocking access to some inappropriate material online. But in the hands of government, blocking software is nothing more than censorship in a box.

The ACLU believes that government has a necessary role to play in promoting universal Internet access. But that role should focus on expanding, not restricting, access to online speech.

Reno v. ACLU: A Momentous Decision

Our vision of an uncensored Internet was clearly shared by the U.S. Supreme Court when it struck down the 1996 Communications Decency Act (CDA), a federal law that outlawed "indecent" communications online.

Ruling unanimously in *Reno v. ACLU*, the Court declared the Internet to be a free speech zone, deserving of at least as much First Amendment protection as that afforded to books, newspapers and magazines. The government, the Court said, can no more restrict a person's access to words or images on the Internet than it could be allowed to snatch a book out of a reader's hands in the library, or cover over a statue of a nude in a museum.

The nine Justices were clearly persuaded by the unique nature of the medium itself, citing with approval the lower federal court's conclusion that the Internet is "the most participatory form of mass speech yet developed," entitled to "the highest protection from governmental intrusion." The Internet, the Court concluded, is like "a vast library including millions of readily available and indexed publications," the content of which "is as diverse as human thought."

Blocking Software: For Parents, Not the Government

In striking down the CDA on constitutional grounds, the Supreme Court emphasized that if a statute burdens adult speech – as any censorship law must – it "is unacceptable if less restrictive alternatives were available."

Commenting on the availability of user-based blocking software as a possible alternative, the Court concluded that the use of such software was appropriate for *parents*. Blocking software, the Court wrote, is a "reasonably effective method by which parents can prevent their children from accessing material which the *parents* believe is inappropriate." [Emphasis in the original]

The rest of the Court's decision firmly holds that government censorship of the Internet violates the First Amendment, and that holding applies to government use of blocking software just as it applied when the Court struck down the CDA's criminal ban.

In the months since that ruling, the blocking software market has experienced explosive growth, as parents exercise their prerogative to guide their childrens' Internet experience. According to analysts at International Data Corporation, a technology consulting firm, software makers sold an estimated $14 million in blocking software last year, and over the next three years, sales of blocking products are expected to grow to more than $75 million.

An increasing number of city and county library boards have recently forced libraries to install blocking programs, over the objections of the American Library Association and library patrons, and the use of blocking software in libraries is fast becoming the biggest free speech controversy since the legal challenge to the CDA.

How Does Blocking Software Work?

The best known Internet platform is the World Wide Web, which allows users to search for and retrieve information stored in remote computers. The Web currently contains over 100 million documents, with thousands added each day. Because of the ease with which material can be added and manipulated, the content on existing Web sites is constantly changing. Links from one computer to another and from one document to another across the Internet are what unify the Web into a single body of knowledge, and what makes the Web unique.

To gain access to the information available on the Web, a person uses a Web "browser" – software such as Netscape Navigator or Microsoft's Internet Explorer – to display, print and download documents. Each document on the Web has an address that allows users to find and retrieve it.

A variety of systems allow users of the Web to search for particular information among all of the public sites that are part of the Web. Services such as Yahoo, Magellan, Alta Vista, Webcrawler, Lycos and Infoseek provide tools called "search engines." Once a user has accessed the search service she simply types a word or string of words as a search request and the search engine provides a list of matching sites.

Blocking software is configured to hide or prevent access to certain Internet sites. Most blocking software comes packaged in a box and can be purchased at retail computer stores. It is installed on individual and/or networked computers that have access to the Internet, and works in conjunction with a Web browser to block information and sites on the Internet that would otherwise be available.

What Kind of Speech is Being Blocked?

Most blocking software prevents access to sites based on criteria provided by the vendor. To conduct site-based blocking, a vendor establishes criteria to identify specified categories of speech on the Internet and configures the blocking software to block sites containing those categories of speech. Some Internet blocking software blocks as few as six categories of information, while others block many more.

Blocked categories may include hate speech, criminal activity, sexually explicit speech, "adult" speech, violent speech, religious speech, and even sports and entertainment.

Using its list of criteria, the software vendor compiles and maintains lists of "unacceptable" sites. Some software vendors employ individuals who browse the Internet for sites to block. Others use automated searching tools to identify which sites to block. These methods may be used in combination. (Examples of blocked sites can be found below and in the Appendix.)

Typical examples of blocked words and letters include "xxx," which blocks out Superbowl XXX sites; "breast," which blocks website and discussion groups about breast cancer; and the consecutive letters "s," "e" and "x," which block sites containing the words "sexton" and "Mars exploration," among many others. Some software blocks categories of expression along blatantly ideological lines, such as information about feminism or gay and lesbian issues. Yet most websites offering opposing views on these issues are not blocked. For example, the same software does not block sites expressing opposition to homosexuality and women working outside the home.

Clearly, the answer to blocking based on ideological viewpoint is not more blocking, any more than the answer to unpopular speech is to prevent everyone from speaking, because then no viewpoint of any kind will be heard. The American Family Association, a conservative religious organization, recently learned this lesson when it found that CyberPatrol, a popular brand of blocking software, had placed AFA on its "Cybernot" list because of the group's opposition to homosexuality.

AFA's site was blocked under the category "intolerance," defined as "pictures or text advocating prejudice or discrimination against any race, color, national origin, religion, disability or handicap, gender or sexual orientation. Any picture or text that elevates one group over another. Also includes intolerance jokes or slurs." Other "Cybernot" categories include "violence/profanity," "nudity," "sexual acts," "satanic/cult," and "drugs/drug culture."

In a May 28th news release excoriating CyberPatrol, AFA said, "CyberPatrol has elected to block the AFA website with their filter because we have simply taken an opposing viewpoint to the political and cultural agenda of the homosexual rights movement." As one AFA spokesman told reporters, "Basically we're being blocked for free speech."

The AFA said they are planning to appeal the blocking decision at a June 9th meeting of CyberPatrol's Cybernot Oversight Committee, but expressed doubt that the decision would be overturned. The conservative Family Research Council also joined in the fight, saying they had "learned that the Gay Lesbian Alliance Against Defamation (GLAAD) is a charter member of Cyber Patrol's oversight committee," and that "it was pressure by GLAAD that turned CyberPatrol around."

Until now, AFA, FRC and similar groups had been strong advocates for filtering software, and AFA has even assisted in the marketing of another product, X-Stop. AFA has said that they still support blocking but believe their group was unfairly singled out.

Indeed, as the AFA and others have learned, there is no avoiding the fact that somebody out there is making judgments about what is offensive and controversial, judgments that may not coincide with their own. The First Amendment exists precisely to protect the most offensive and controversial speech from government suppression. If blocking software is made mandatory in schools and libraries, that "somebody" making the judgments becomes the government.

To Block or Not to Block: You Decide

According to a recent story in The Washington Post, a software vendor's "own test of a sample of Web sites found that the software allowed pornographic sites to get through and blocked 57 sites that did not contain anything objectionable."

And in a current lawsuit in Virginia over the use of blocking software in libraries, the ACLU argues that the software blocks "a wide variety of other Web sites that contain valuable and constitutionally protected speech, such as the entire Web site of Glide Memorial United Methodist Church, located in San Francisco, California, and the entire Web site of The San Francisco Chronicle."

Following are real-world examples of the kind of speech that has been found to be inaccessible in libraries where blocking software is installed. Read through them – or look at them online – and then decide for yourself: Do you want the government telling you whether you can access these sites in the library?

www.afa.net

The American Family Association is a non-profit group founded in 1977 by the Rev. Donald Wildmon. According to their website, the AFA "stands for traditional family values, focusing primarily on the influence of television and other media – including pornography – on our society."

www.cmu.edu

Banned Books On-Line offers the full text of over thirty books that have been the object of censorship or censorship attempts, from James Joyce's Ulysses to Little Red Riding Hood.

www.quaker.org

The Religious Society of Friends describes itself as "an Alternative Christianity which emphasizes the personal experience of God in one's life." Their site boasts the slogan, "Proud to Be Censored by X-Stop, a popular brand of blocking software."

www.safersex.org

The Safer Sex Page includes brochures about safer sex, HIV transmission, and condoms, as well as resources for health educators and counselors. X-Stop, the software that blocks these pages, does not block the "The Safest Sex Home Page," which promotes abstinence before marriage as the only protection against sexually transmitted diseases.

www.iatnet.com/aauw

The American Association of University Women Maryland provides information about its activities to promote equity for women. The Web site discusses AAUW's leadership role in civil rights issues; work and family issues such as pay equity, family and medical leave, and dependent care; sex discrimination; and reproductive rights.

www.sfgate.com/columnists/morse

Rob Morse, an award-winning columnist for The San Francisco Examiner, has written more than four hundred columns on a variety of issues ranging from national politics, homelessness, urban violence, computer news, and the Superbowl, to human cloning. Because his section is considered off limits, the entire www.sfgate.com site is blocked to viewers.

http://www.youth.org/yao/docs/books.html

Books for Gay and Lesbian Teens/Youth provides information about books of interest to gay and lesbian youth. The site was created by Jeremy Meyers, an 18-year-old senior in high school who lives in New York City. X-Stop, the software that blocks this page, does not block web pages condemning homosexuality.

www.sfgate.com

This website is the home of Sergio Arau, a Mexican painter, composer, and musician, who has been called one of Mexico's most diversely talented artists. He has recorded several successful compact disks, including a recent release on Sony Records, and his paintings have been exhibited in numerous museums and galleries, including the Museo Rufino Tamayo in Mexico City.

www.spectacle.org

The Ethical Spectacle is a free online magazine that addresses issues at the intersection of ethics, law, and politics in American life. Jonathan Wallace, the creator of the site, is also co-author with Mark Mangan of Sex, Laws, and Cyberspace, which received much critical praise and is widely available in libraries and book stores around the country.

In addition to these examples, a growing body of research compiled by educators, public interest organizations and other interested groups demonstrates the extent to which this software inappropriately blocks valuable, protected speech, and does not effectively block the sites they claim to block. A list of these studies can be found in Appendix I.

Teaching Responsibility: Solutions that Work . . .

Instead of requiring unconstitutional blocking software, schools and libraries should establish content-neutral rules about when and how young people should use the Internet, and hold educational seminars on responsible use of the Internet.

For instance, schools could request that Internet access be limited to school-related work and develop carefully worded acceptable use policies (AUPs), that provide instructions for parents, teachers, students, librarians and patrons on use of the Internet. (See Appendix III for information about AUPs and other alternatives to blocking software.)

Successful completion of a seminar similar to a driver's education course could be required of minors who seek Internet privileges in the classroom or library. Such seminars could emphasize the dangers of disclosing personally identifiable information such as one's address, communicating with strangers about personal or intimate matters, or relying on inaccurate resources on the Net.

Whether the use of blocking software is mandatory or not, parents should always be informed that blind reliance on blocking programs cannot effectively safeguard children.

Libraries can and should take other actions that are more protective of online free speech principles. For instance, libraries can publicize and provide links to particular sites that have been recommended for children.

Not all solutions are necessarily "high tech." To avoid unwanted viewing by passers-by, for instance, libraries can place privacy screens around Internet access terminals in ways that minimize public view. Libraries can also impose content-neutral time limits on Internet use.

These positive approaches work much better than restrictive software that works only when students are using school or library computers, and teaches no critical thinking skills. After all, sooner or later students graduate to the real world, or use a computer without blocking software. An educational program could teach students how to use the technology to find information quickly and efficiently, and how to exercise their own judgment to assess the quality and reliability of information they receive.

. . . and Don't Work

In an effort to avoid installing blocking software, some libraries have instituted a "tap on the shoulder" policy that is, in many ways, more intrusive and unconstitutional than a computer program. This authorizes librarians to peer at the patron's computer screen and tap anyone on the shoulder who is viewing "inappropriate" material.

The ACLU recently contacted a library in Newburgh, New York to advise against a proposed policy that would permit librarians to stop patrons from accessing "offensive" and "racially or sexually inappropriate material." In a letter to the Newburgh Board of Education, the ACLU wrote: "The Constitution protects dirty words, racial epithets, and sexually explicit speech, even though that speech may be offensive to some." The letter also noted that the broad language of the policy would allow a librarian to prevent a patron from viewing on the Internet such classic works of fiction as Chaucer's Canterbury Tales and Mark Twain's Adventures of Huckleberry Finn, and such classic works of art as Manet's Olympia and Michelangelo's David.

"This thrusts the librarian into the role of Big Brother and allows for arbitrary and discriminatory enforcement since each librarian will have a different opinion about what is offensive," the ACLU said.

The First Amendment prohibits librarians from directly censoring protected speech in the library, just as it prevents indirect censorship through blocking software.

Battling Big Brother in the Library

In Loudoun County, Virginia, the ACLU is currently involved in the first court challenge to the use of blocking software in a library. Recently, the judge in that case forcefully rejected a motion to dismiss the lawsuit, saying that the government had "misconstrued the nature of the Internet" and warning that Internet blocking requires the strictest level of constitutional scrutiny. The case is now set to go to trial this fall.

Earlier this year, the ACLU was involved in a local controversy over the mandatory use of Internet blocking programs in California's public libraries. County officials had decided to use a blocking program called "Bess" on every library Internet terminal, despite an admission by Bess's creators that it was impossible to customize the program to filter only material deemed "harmful to minors" by state law.

After months of negotiation, the ACLU warned the county that it would take legal action if officials did not remove Internet blocking software from public library computers. Ultimately, the library conceded that the filters presented an unconstitutional barrier to patrons seeking access to materials including legal opinions, medical information, political commentary, art, literature, information from women's organizations, and even portions of the ACLU Freedom Network website.

Today, under a new policy, the county provides a choice of an unfiltered or a filtered computer to both adult and minor patrons. No parental consent will be required for minors to access unfiltered computers.

The ACLU has also advocated successfully against mandatory blocking software in libraries in San Jose and in Santa Clara County, California. The ACLU continues to monitor the use of blocking software in many libraries across the nation, including communities in Massachusetts, Texas, Illinois, Ohio and Pennsylvania.

The Fight in Congress: Marshaling the Cyber-Troops Against Censorship

In February of this year, Senator John McCain (R-AZ) introduced the "Internet School Filtering Act," a law that requires all public libraries and schools to use blocking software in order to qualify for "e-rate," a federal funding program to promote universal Internet access. An amendment that would have allowed schools and libraries to qualify by presenting their own plan to regulate Internet access – not necessarily by commercial filter – failed in committee.

Another bill sponsored by Senator Dan Coats (R-IN) was dubbed "Son of CDA," because much of it is identical to the ill-fated Communications Decency Act.

The ACLU and others are lobbying against these bills, which have not yet come up for a vote as of this writing.

Censorship in the States: A Continuing Battle

Federal lawmakers are not the only politicians jumping on the censorship bandwagon. In the last three years, at least 25 states have considered or passed

Internet censorship laws. This year, at least seven states are considering bills that require libraries and/or schools to use blocking software.

These censorship laws have not held up to constitutional scrutiny. Federal district courts in New York, Georgia and Virginia have found Internet censorship laws unconstitutional on First Amendment grounds in challenges brought by the ACLU. In April, the ACLU filed a challenge to an Internet censorship law in New Mexico that is remarkably similar to the failed New York law.

Conclusion

The advent of new forms of communication technology is always a cause for public anxiety and unease. This was as true for the printing press and the telephone as it was for the radio and the television. But the constitutional ideal is immutable regardless of the medium: a free society is based on the principle that each and every individual has the right to decide what kind of information he or she wants – or does not want – to receive or create. Once you allow the government to censor material you don't like, you cede to it the power to censor something you do like – even your own speech.

Censorship, like poison gas, can be highly effective when the wind is blowing the right way. But the wind has a way of shifting, and sooner or later, it blows back upon the user. Whether it comes in a box or is accessed online, in the hands of the government, blocking software is toxic to a democratic society.

Questions and Answers about Blocking Software

In the interest of "unblocking" the truth, here are answers to some of the questions the ACLU most often encounters on the issue of blocking software:

Q: Why does it matter whether Internet sites are blocked at the library when people who want to see them can just access them at home?

A: According to a recent Nielsen Survey, 45 percent of Internet users go to public libraries for Internet access. For users seeking controversial or personal information, the library is often their only opportunity for privacy. A Mormon teenager in Utah seeking information about other religions may not want a parent in the home, or a teacher at school, looking over her shoulder as she surfs the web.

Q: What about library policies that allow patrons to request that certain sites be unblocked?

A: The stigma of requesting access to a blocked site deters many people from making that request. Library patrons may be deterred from filling out a form seeking access, because the sites they wish to visit contain sensitive information. For instance, a woman seeking to access the Planned Parenthood website to find out about birth control may feel embarrassed about justifying the request to a librarian.

Q: But as long as a library patron can ask for a site to be unblocked, no one's speech is really being censored, right?

A: Wrong. Web providers who want their speech to reach library patrons have no way to request that their site be unblocked in thousands of libraries around the country. They fear patrons will be stigmatized for requesting that the site be unblocked, or simply won't bother to make the request. If public libraries around the country continue to use blocking software, speakers will be forced to self-censor in order to avoid being blocked in libraries.

Q: Isn't it true that librarians can use blocking software in the same way they select books for circulation?

A: The unique nature of the Internet means that librarians do not have to consider the limitations of shelf space in providing access to online material. In a recent ruling concerning the use of blocking software in Virginia libraries, a federal judge agreed with the analogy of the Internet as "a collection of encyclopedias from which defendants [the government] have laboriously redacted [or crossed out] portions deemed unfit for library patrons."

Q: Doesn't blocking software help a librarian control what children see online?

A: The ability to choose which software is installed does not empower a school board or librarian to determine what is "inappropriate for minors." Instead, that determination is made by a software vendor who regards the lists of blocked sites as secret, proprietary information.

Q: Why shouldn't librarians be involved in preventing minors from accessing inappropriate material on the Internet?

A: It is the domain of parents, not librarians, to oversee their children's library use. This approach preserves the integrity of the library as a storehouse of ideas available to all regardless of age or income. As stated by the American Library Association's Office of Intellectual Freedom: "Parents and only parents have the right and responsibility to restrict their own children's access – and only their own children's access – to library resources, including the Internet. Librarians do not serve *in loco parentis*."

Q: What do librarians themselves think about blocking software?

A: The overwhelming majority of librarians are opposed to the mandatory use of blocking software. However some, under pressure from individuals or local officials, have installed blocking software. The ALA has a Library Bill of Rights, which maintains that filters should not be used "to block access to constitutionally protected speech."

Q: Isn't blocking software an inexpensive way for libraries to monitor Internet use?

A: While parents may be able to purchase a blocking program for around $40, the cost for library systems is much greater. One library has estimated the initial installation of blocking software at $8,000 plus an additional $3,000 a year to maintain. As the court noted in ongoing case in Virginia case, "it costs a library more to restrict the content of its collection by means of blocking software than it does for the library to offer unrestricted access to all Internet publications."

Q: Are libraries required to use blocking software in order to avoid criminal liability for providing minors access to speech that may not be protected by the Constitution?

A: No. The First Amendment prohibits imposing criminal or civil liability on librarians merely for providing minors with access to the Internet. The knowledge that some websites on the Internet may contain "harmful" matter is not sufficient grounds for prosecution. In fact, an attempt to avoid any liability by installing blocking software or otherwise limiting minors' access to the Internet would, itself, violate the First Amendment.

Q: Would libraries that do not use blocking software be liable for sexual harassment in the library?

A: No. Workplace sexual harassment laws apply only to employees, not to patrons. The remote possibility that a library employee might inadvertently view an objectionable site does not constitute sexual harassment under current law.

Q: Can't blocking programs be fixed so they block only illegal speech that is not protected by the Constitution?

A: There is simply no way for a computer software program to make distinctions between protected and unprotected speech. This is not a design flaw that may be "fixed" at some future point but a simple human truth. (For more on this subject, see Appendix II.)

Q: What if blocking software is only made mandatory for kids?

A: Even if only minors are forced to use blocking programs, constitutional problems remain. The Supreme Court has agreed that minors have rights too, and the fact that a 15-year-old rather than an 18 year-old seeks access online to valuable information on subjects such as religion or gay and lesbian resources does not mean that the First Amendment no longer applies. In any case, it is impossible for a computer program to distinguish what is appropriate for different age levels, or the age of the patron using the computer.

Q: Is using blocking software at schools any different than using it in public libraries?

A: Unlike libraries, schools do act in place of parents, and play a role in teaching civic values. Students do have First Amendment rights, however, and blocking software is inappropriate, especially for junior and high school students.

In addition, because the software often blocks valuable information while allowing access to objectionable material, parents are given a false sense of security about what their children are viewing. A less restrictive – and more effective – alternative is the establishment of content-neutral "Acceptable Use Policies" (AUPs). (See Appendix III).

Q: Despite all these problems, isn't blocking software worth it if it keeps some pornography from reaching kids?

A: Even though sexually explicit sites only make up a very small percentage of content on the Internet, it is impossible for any one program to block out every conceivable web page with "inappropriate" material.

When blocking software is made mandatory, adults as well as minors are prevented from communicating online, even in schools. According to a recent news story in the Los Angeles Times, a restrictive blocking program at a California school district meant coaches couldn't access the University of Notre Dame's website, and math instructors were cut off from information about Wall Street because of a block on references to money and finance.

Q: Does this mean that parents can't use blocking software in the home?

A: No. The ACLU believes that parents have a right to use – or not use – whatever blocking software they choose.

Appendix I

Following are brief descriptions of some recent studies and reports addressing specific problems with blocking software.

http://www2.epic.org/reports/filter_report.html

Faulty Filters: How Content Filters Block Access to Kid-Friendly Information on the Internet, reviewed the impact of a "family-friendly" search engine from the NetShepherd Corporation. The report, released by the Electronic Privacy Information Center (EPIC), compared 100 search results using the unfiltered AltaVista search engine and using AltaVista in conjunction with the NetShepherd search engine. EPIC found that NetShepherd typically blocked access to 95-99 percent of material available on the net that might be of interest to young people – including the American Red Cross, the San Diego Zoo, and the Smithsonian Institution. At the time EPIC's report was written, Net Shepherd claimed that it had reviewed "97% of the English language sites on the Web," a claim that was later retracted.

http://www.glaad.org

Access Denied, a report by the Gay and Lesbian Alliance Against Defamation (GLAAD) concludes that most blocking products categorize and block all information about gays and lesbians in the same manner that they block sexually explicit and pornographic material. For instance, the report noted that the rating program SurfWatch blocked online sites such as the International Association of Gay Square Dance Clubs, the Queer Resources Directory, the Lesbian/Gay/Bisexual Association of the University of California at Berkeley, and the Maine Gay Network.

http://www.spectacle.org/cwp/

Blacklisted by CyberPatrol, a report by the Censorware Project, found that CyberPatrol software blocks tens of thousands of web pages with innocent content, simply because a few users linked to more sexually explicit web pages. The report also shows that wrongfully blocked sites are often inaccurately described by CyberPatrol. For instance, "Full Nude Sex Acts" was used to describe websites for the U.S. Army Corps of Engineers Construction Engineering Research Laboratories, Cafe Haven at Brigham Young University, a server at the Japan Institute of Technology in Chiba, Japan, and the Department Of Computer Science at Queen Mary Westfield College. None of these websites were found to contain explicit material.

The **Internet Free Expression Alliance**, of which the ACLU is a founding member, is an excellent resource for more links to studies, background information and news articles on Internet censorship. The website is **http://www.ifea.net**.

Appendix III: Alternatives to Blocking Software

Acceptable Use Policies (AUPs)

Public Library Internet Access Policies
http://www.ci.oswego.or.us/library/poli.htm

Public Library Internet Access Policies is a website created by Oregon's Lake Oswego Public Library. Containing a comprehensive collection of library AUPs, its purpose is "to provide objective, unbiased information for public librarians about Internet access policies."

K-12 Acceptable Use Policies
http://www.erehwon.com/k12aup/index.html K-12

Acceptable Use Policies is a website created by Information Technology Consultant Nancy Willard. Its purpose is to assist school districts in the development of effective Internet policies and practices. It contains a legal and educational analysis of K-12 AUPs, as well as a sample letter to parents and a sample student account agreement.

Librarian and Educator-Recommended Sites

Great Sites
http://www.ala.org/parentspage/greatsites/amazing.html

700+ Great Sites: Amazing, Spectacular, Mysterious, Colorful Web Sites for Kids and the Adults Who Care About Them is a website maintained by the American Library Association. Compiled by the Association's Children and Technology Committee, it recommends websites covering the areas of Arts and Entertainment, Literature and Language, People Past and Present, Planet Earth and Beyond, and Science and Technology.

Internet Public Library
http://www.ipl.org

The Internet Public Library describes itself as "the first library of and for the Internet community." Created in 1995 by a University of Michigan Library Studies class, the IPL is now a permanent, staffed institution. Its collection includes both a teen division and a youth division of suggested age-appropriate websites.

Brochure for Parents

Child Safety on the Information Highway
http://www.safekids.com/child_safety.htm

Safe Kids Online is a brochure published by the National Center for Missing and Exploited Children that is available online as well as in printed form. It gives parents accurate information about risks that children and teenagers may be exposed to on the Internet, and encourages parents to educate their children to be "street smart" rather than to restrict their Internet access. The brochure includes a set of guidelines for parents, and a section for kids called "My Rules for Online Safety."

The Cyber-Library: Legal and Policy Issues Facing Public Libraries in the High-Tech Era

National Coalition Against Censorship

Introduction

Since the inception of the public library movement in the mid-19th century, public libraries have occupied a unique and critical role in American society. To generations of Americans—native born and immigrants, rich and poor—public libraries have provided free access to resources that stimulate the mind, nourish the imagination, and connect individuals to people and events outside the boundaries of their own experiences. Libraries have been conduits for information about jobs, government programs and community services. As public spaces, they have served both as safe havens for private reflection and as meeting places for community functions.

In all these various roles and for all these reasons, public libraries in the United States and around the world have promoted values and experiences that are fundamental to a democratic society, offering equal access to essential tools for informed participation in the political process. The First Amendment to the United States Constitution[1] guarantees "public access to discussion, debate and

[1] The First Amendment provides, in relevant part, that "Congress shall make no law . . . abridging the freedom of speech. . . ." While legal analysis in this paper is based on law in the United States, much of the policy discussion is relevant beyond its borders.

United States Constitution[1] guarantees "public access to discussion, debate and the dissemination of information and ideas"[2] and the public library has been recognized as a "quintessential locus" for such access.[3] In the European community, too, public libraries are acknowledged as bulwarks of an open, equal society.[4]

The traditional roles of public libraries and librarians are under new scrutiny, however, as computers and the Internet challenge familiar notions of community and defy common assumptions about what, how, where and with whom we learn and communicate. To remain viable public institutions, libraries—and the communities that support them—must revisit and clarify their mission, identifying and capitalizing on the services they are uniquely positioned to offer and exploiting the technology to best advantage. The task is complicated by the fact that the landscape continues to change as the technology evolves and becomes available in more and more households [5] and at alternative access points like free-standing information kiosks and community technology centers.[6]

---

[1] The First Amendment provides, in relevant part, that "Congress shall make no law . . .abridging the freedom of speech. . . ." While legal analysis in this paper is based on law in the United States, much of the policy discussion is relevant beyond its borders.

[2] *First National Bank of Boston v. Bellotti*, 435 U.S. 765, 783 (1978), as quoted in *Board of Education v. Pico*, 457 U.S. 858, 866 (1982).

[3] *Kreimer v. Bureau of Police for the Town of Morristown*, 958 F.2d 1242, 1254 (3rd Cir. 1992).

[4] EU Parliament, Committee on Culture, Youth, Education and the Media, THE REPORT ON THE GREEN PAPER ON THE ROLE OF LIBRARIES IN THE MODERN WORLD (1998)(Rapporteur: Mrs. Mirja Ryynaen) <http://www.lib.hel.fi/skye/english/publications/report.htm>. The report emphasizes that "without . . services [of public libraries] society cannot be democratic, open and transparent because it cannot be assumed that all citizens will have acquired a wide range of material. Investing in libraries means investing in democracy and equality."

[5] It is predicted that 33% of all households in the United States will be online by the end of 1999. International Data Corporation, *Executive Insight, IDC Predictions '99: The "Real" Internet Emerges* <http://www.idc.com> (visited January 1999). The Internet audience is gradually becoming more inclusive and more diverse. *See, e.g.,* Pew Center for People and the Press, THE INTERNET NEWS AUDIENCE GOES ORDINARY (January 1999)<http://www.people-press.org/tech98sum.htm>; John Simons, *Is the Web Political Poll Reliable?* WALL STREET JOURNAL, April 13, 1999 (reporting Harris Black International Ltd. Survey). However, there remain troubling disparities in both ownership and use, as discussed at page 4.

[6] The role of community networks and information kiosks as participants in the information infrastructure is described in Redmond Kathleen Molz and Phyllis Dain, CIVIC SPACE / CYBERSPACE (MIT Press 1999) (hereafter CIVIC SPACE / CYBERSPACE).These alternative access points compete with the library for Internet users. Competitive pressures also come from the private sector. Super bookstores like Barnes

---

Most libraries in the United States are now connected to the Internet, and some have moved beyond connectivity in ways that complement and supplement existing programs and services. The Internet contains a nearly infinite array of material from sources around the globe, some of it reliable, some not. Many librarians are at the front lines of technology training, educating new computer users in search techniques and helping them evaluate the relevance and validity of online information. Some libraries are becoming Internet "publishers," often as part of a network that creates a virtual public space to reinvigorate a real world community. Some are also using the full potential of the technology, including e-mail and chat functions, as a magnet to attract new patrons and introduce them to a wide variety of services and materials, including books. These substantive programs and outreach efforts are especially significant for underserved populations who, at this point—and perhaps for some time to come—might otherwise be denied the benefits of the new technology.

Sadly, these positive developments are often overlooked, at least in the popular media, in favor of campaigns to restrict or limit access to the Internet, based on concerns about material with explicit sexual or violent content.[7] Most local libraries have developed policies and procedures to handle these issues without censorship, but calls for mandatory filtering and other forms of restrictions continue to engage the public discourse and to threaten library users' ability to exploit the full potential of the medium. The economics of the new technology also pose serious issues. The cost of hardware, software, upgrades, training and staff necessary to move beyond connectivity to provide meaningful access and user support is a significant barrier for many libraries, forcing them to look for new sources of funds and to rethink priorities.

The challenges are significant: Will the Internet become an effective force for promoting the free flow of information and ideas, or an excuse for restricting it?

---

and Noble offer alternative "public" spaces as well as a variety of programs like children's story hours that are also offered by public libraries. However, the book buying audience also tends to be supportive of libraries. Benton Foundation, BUILDINGS, BOOKS AND BYTES: LIBRARIES AND COMMUNITIES IN THE DIGITAL AGE (1996) at 14, 21-22.

[7] A recent report revealed that sex crimes regarding children and the Web were featured in one of every four articles surveyed and that "disturbing issues" relating to the Web and the family showed up in two of every three such articles. At the same time, the press failed to depict librarians (among others) as resources for support for concerned parents. Annenberg Public Policy Center of the University of Pennsylvania, THE INTERNET AND THE FAMILY: THE VIEW FROM THE PARENTS, THE VIEW FROM THE PRESS (1999) <http://appcpenn.org/internet>.

How can the library secure its role as the facilitator and defender of free thought and inquiry? In planning for both the short-term and the long-term needs of local libraries, decision-makers face a number of important issues:

- What are the current roles of the library in the community? What segments of the community use the library and how do they use it? What are the special needs of minors? Of new Americans? Of underserved populations?

- What roles can and should the library play in the future and how can technology be used to support and enhance those roles? Taking into account the availability of Internet access elsewhere in the community—in schools, other public outlets, and in homes—should the library focus or prioritize its electronic resources? If so, how? Research and information gathering? Adult learning? Entertainment? What programs and services are necessary to support these uses?

- What is the library's obligation to provide training in effective use of the technology? How can the library respond to the difficulties of assessing the reliability of information on the Internet?

- What are the risks and benefits of Internet use for different populations and what policies and programs should the library adopt to help patrons use the medium wisely? How can these policies be shaped consistent with the First Amendment and the values of privacy and anonymity? What are the appropriate roles for library staff, parents and others in making decisions about minors' access?

- What hardware, software and other electronic resources (for example, commercial databases) will be needed to implement the library's goals and objectives? What are the associated staff and maintenance costs? What will be the bottom line and where will the funds come from?

This paper is intended as a resource for communities seeking to take advantage of the benefits of technology without sacrificing free speech and inquiry. Part I of the full paper (available from the National Coalition Against Censorship) offers an overview of the ways in which libraries are using the Internet to serve and engage their communities. Part II (which is excerpted here) addresses efforts to censor Internet use in libraries and the implications of First Amendment jurisprudence. It examines some of the concerns raised by censorship advocates and summarizes libraries' responses to these efforts. Finally, Part III of the full paper explores the overall impact on access to information as libraries develop and fund technology plans.

Efforts to Censor the Internet in Public Libraries

A key policy issue affecting the ability of libraries and their patrons to exploit the full potential of the medium is the debate over restricting access to the Internet. Like other innovations in communications, the Internet revives old fears about the power of images and words and raises important questions about the ownership and control of information. The latter issue, beyond the scope of this paper, is at the heart of discussions over changes in copyright law and proposals for commercial database protections.[8] The former is tied to more direct and familiar forms of censorship.

Concerns about violent and sexually explicit material and, in particular the effects on children, have spawned numerous proposals for government regulation of Internet content. These include legislation imposing "upstream" restrictions on the transmission of material as well as mandates for "downstream" controls—filtering and blocking software to limit user access at public institutions. Legislation currently pending at both state and federal levels would require schools and libraries to filter the Internet as a condition for receipt of government funds for technology,[9] and the focus on Internet content control has supported a thriving industry devoted to developing and marketing filtering software.

Proposals directed at e-mail and chat in public libraries are based on similar rationales about the need to protect minors. Indeed, some believe that e-mail and chat pose particular risks as venues for online enticement, and because, more often than other Internet uses, these functions elicit "spam," unsolicited bulk e-mail that may include sexually explicit teasers. In its preliminary report, *Kids on the Internet: The Problems and Perils of Cyberspace*, the National Commission

---

[8]Because of the importance to libraries, the American Library Association was a key player in discussions about the Digital Millennium Copyright Act, P.L. 105-304, and the Copyright Term Extension Act, P.L. 105-278. *See also* testimony from the American Library Association and others on the proposed "Collections of Information Antipiracy Act," and <http://www.ala.org/washoff.primer.html> and <http://www.ala.org/washoff/neal.html>.

[9] For a discussion of this legislation, *see* pages 14-15. For an analysis of earlier legislative efforts to impose access restrictions on the Internet and other media, *see, e.g.*, National Coalition Against Censorship, CENSORSHIP'S TOOLS DU JOUR: V-CHIPS, TV RATINGS, PICS AND INTERNET FILTERS (March 1998) <http://www.ncac.org/ resources.html>.

---

on Libraries and Information Science recommended that libraries limit children's chat to specifically approved moderated chat groups and designated interactive sites.[10] Some would ban chat and e-mail from public institutions altogether.

In the few cases decided thus far,the courts have rebuffed efforts to censor the Internet, finding that the government did not meet the high level of justification required by the First Amendment.[11] However each of these courts assumed – at least for purposes of litigation – that the government had a "compelling" interest in protecting minors. Yet, as discussed below, the evidence of harm from Internet access at public institutions is at best equivocal, and the blunt-edged approach advocated by pro-censorship advocates ignores the individualized needs of children and their parents. Fortunately, most libraries have found ways of balancing the interests of all parties effectively, without censorship. Some of these "less restrictive alternatives" are summarized in this section.

A. First Amendment Principles in Cyberspace

According to the Supreme Court, cyberspace is a free speech zone, and the Internet is thus entitled to the highest level of First Amendment protection. To meet constitutional standards, restrictions on online speech must be both necessary to serve a "compelling interest" and the least restrictive means of doing so.

1. The Constitutionality of "Upstream" Content Restrictions.

In the first case to articulate these principles, *Reno v. ACLU ("Reno I")*,[12] the Supreme Court struck down provisions of the Communications Decency Act[13] that criminalized the knowing transmission and display of "indecent" material to

---

[10] National Commission on Libraries and Information Science, KIDS ON THE INTERNET: THE PROBLEMS AND PERILS OF CYBERSPACE (preliminary report) (January 1998) <http://www.nclis.gov>.

[11] In addition to the cases discussed below, see also *American Civil Liberties Union v. Johnson*, 4 F. Supp.2d 1029 (D.N.M. 1998) (appeal docketed 8/7/98, 10th Cir. No. 98-2199)(upholding First Amendment challenge). *But see Urofsky v. Gilmore*, 167 F.3d 191 (4th Cir. 1999) (rehearing *en banc* granted 6/3/9, 4th Cir. No. 98-1481) (upholding Virginia law restricting state employees access to sexually explicit materials on state computers). Two additional cases, *American Library Association v. Pataki*, 969 F. Supp. 160 (S.D.N.Y. 1997) and *ACLU v. Miller*, 977 F.Supp. 1228 (N.D.Ga. 1997) were decided on other grounds.

[12] *Reno v. American Civil Liberties Union*, 521 U.S. 844 (1997).

[13] The Communications Decency Act (CDA) was passed with little analysis as part of the Telecommunications Act of 1996. *Reno I*, 521 U.S. at 859 and note 24.

---

minors under the age of 18. Although acknowledging a government interest in protecting minors from certain types of sexual content, it held the statute unconstitutional because of its broad reach and its ambiguous language. (What, precisely, is "indecent"?) The combined effect of these infirmities, the Court concluded, would suppress not only unprotected material, but also "much speech that adults have a right to receive and to address to each other," and would be like "burning the house to roast the pig."

Following *Reno I*, Congress passed the Child Online Protection Act (COPA), specifically drafted in an effort to avoid the constitutional pitfalls of the CDA. In a decision that is now on appeal, a federal district court in Philadelphia enjoined enforcement of the statute.[14] It held that the legislation failed the strict scrutiny test in part because it was simply ineffective in solving the alleged problem of minors' access to sexual materials. The Internet transcends national boundaries, and, as a practical matter, the statute could not preclude minors from obtaining sexual materials from foreign sites, which are not subject to U.S. jurisdiction. Nor could it curb enterprising and technologically savvy minors from bypassing mechanisms designed to permit adult-only access. In any event, the court noted, less restrictive and equally effective means to protect children are available, including blocking and filtering software capable of "downstream" regulation of content, regardless of its source.[15]

2. The Constitutionality of "Downstream" Content Restrictions: Blocking and Filtering Internet Access in Public Libraries

Blocking and filtering software suffer from numerous and serious flaws, which have been repeatedly and persuasively documented.[16] Such devices are under-

---

[14] *American Civil Liberties Union v. Reno*, 31 F.Supp. 2d 473 (E.D.Pa. 1999)(appeal docketed 4/26/99, 3d Cir. No. 99-1324). The statute applies only to commercial activities on the World Wide Web containing material deemed harmful to minors, made with knowledge of the character of the material. Restricting access by requiring a credit card or through other means is a defense.

[15] The fact that communications from outside the US are not subject to domestic law is one reason why "upstream" restrictions like the CDA and COPA are inherently ineffective. An expert in the COPA case estimated that about 40% of all Internet content originate outside the U.S. *American Civil Liberties Union v. Reno*, Finding of Fact A 13.

[16] *See, e.g.,* Electronic Information Privacy Center, FAULTY FILTERS: HOW CONTENT FILTERS BLOCK ACCESS TO KID FRIENDLY INFORMATION ON THE INTERNET (1997) <http://www2.epic.org/reports/filter-report.html>. A March 1999 report by the Censorware Project on filtering in Utah public schools and libraries <http://censorware.org/reports/utah/>, showed that users were banned from numerous useful and educational sites, including the Constitution and the Bible.

and over-inclusive, employ subjective judgments, exclude a great deal of useful and harmless information, and often conceal both the criteria for blocking and information about what material is blocked. While individuals are free to block or filter Internet access at home, the use of such technology in public institutions is constitutionally suspect. In *Mainstream Loudoun v. Board of Trustees of the Loudoun County Library*, a federal district court in Virginia, applying the strict scrutiny test, held that the installation of blocking software at all Internet terminals at a local library violated the First Amendment.[17]

Several aspects of the decision are significant for local libraries. First, although the court assumed a compelling interest in minimizing minors' access to sexually explicit content, it found that the policy was not necessary. The library offered no evidence of problems involving minors at its own facility and presented only isolated instances of incidents elsewhere. One of these was successfully resolved by the use of a privacy screen[18] which, in addition to acceptable use policies and educational programs, was a less restrictive option that the library could have implemented, but did not.

Finally, the court found that the library had impermissibly delegated blocking decisions to a private company which censored material based on "secret criteria" that it refused to disclose, even to the library itself. Adult patrons could request that library staff "unblock" a particular site, but the court concluded that the request procedure imposed an unconstitutional burden on library patrons and gave staff unbridled discretion to reject any request.

A second library case, decided without opinion by a California Superior Court, *Kathleen R. v. City of Livermore*,[19] presents the flip side of Mainstream Loudoun: whether a library can be held civilly liable for *declining* to filter the Internet. The plaintiff's 12-year old son had allegedly downloaded pornography, and she claimed that the library was maintaining a public nuisance and violating other state laws. The court dismissed the claims,[20] and the case is now on appeal.

---

[17] *Mainstream Loudoun v. Board of Trustees of the Loundoun County Library*, 24 F. Supp.2d 552 (E.D. Va 1998).

[18] Privacy screens physically shield computer users, preventing non-users from viewing the screen.

[19] No. V-015266, California Superior Court, Alameda County, Eastern Division

[20] In an amicus brief, the ACLU of Northern California and others argued that blocking would constitute an unlawful prior restraint on speech and that two sections of the CDA (not at issue in *Reno* I) immunized the library from civil liability based on its role as a "provider" of content originating with a third party. The latter argument relied on the Fourth Circuit decision in *Zeran v. America Online, Inc.*, 958 F. Supp. 1124 (E.D. Va.

3. A Constitutional Right to Chat?

So far, no court has addressed the constitutional dimensions of the right to chat and e-mail in public institutions.[21] Libraries that have never used Internet Relay Chat ("IRC") software and have never offered e-mail are probably not constitutionally required to so do, any more than a library with a full complement of books is required to buy audiotapes. But increasingly, the ability to chat, to send and receive e-mail, and to participate in newsgroups does not depend on specialized software or knowledge of distinct Internet protocols: all that is required is access to the World Wide Web.[22] And First Amendment principles suggest that having made the decision to offer web access, libraries may not be able to limit access to these communications functions unless the strict scrutiny test is met.

Under the First Amendment, even apparently neutral rules—for example, a blanket ban on all chat—are suspect if the "predominant intent" behind the regulation is to discriminate against controversial or unpopular ideas or viewpoints. "The government's *purpose* is the controlling consideration."[23] Thus, if the clear intent is to restrict access to sexual material, limits on chat and

---

1997). Zeran had sued AOL for defamation based on comments posted to an AOL bulletin board. The court applied the immunity provisions of the CDA even though AOL had known of Zeran's objections and had failed to act. These sections may also provide libraries with immunity from criminal liability under state "harmful to minors' statutes. For a discussion of this and related issues under state law, *see* Memorandum to Freedom to Read Foundation from Jenner and Block, *Civil and Criminal Liabilities for Libraries* (August 1998) <http://www.ala.org/alaorg/oif/civil_jb.html>.

[21] A blanket ban on e-mail and chat was part of the restrictive policy adopted in Loudoun County. Finding that the filtering requirement "permeat[ed]" the entire policy, the court did not consider either the chat ban or the requirement that computers be installed near and in full view of the library staff. *Mainstream Loudoun* 24 F. Supp. at 570.

[22] The Internet offers several methods of communication and information retrieval, utilizing several different Internet protocols. The protocols originally developed for e-mail, for real time communications (such as Internet Rely Chat) and newsgroups are distinct from HTTP (hyper-text transfer protocol), the protocol for the World Wide Web. Previously, functions using protocols other than HTTP could be accessed from the web only by more sophisticated users or those with specialized software. However, web-based chat rooms, e-mail and newsgroups utilizing HTTP or with a web interface are now common. *See American Civil Liberties Union v. Reno*, No. 98-5591 (E.D.Pa. February 1, 1999), Finding of Fact A8; Janelle Brown, *A Kinder, Gentler Usenet*, SALON MAGAZINE (September 15, 1998) <http://www.salonmagazine.com/21st/feature/1998/09/15feature.html>.

[23] *Ward v. Rock Against Racism*, 491 U.S. 781, 791 (1989). (Citation omitted; emphasis supplied).

---

e-mail may fail to pass constitutional muster for many of the same reasons that the courts have invalidated other approaches to controlling Internet use.[24]

4. Censorship Through Funding Restrictions

Legislation currently pending in Congress would mandate the use of blocking and filtering software by libraries and schools that take advantage of the federal "E-Rate"("education rate"),[25] a discounted rate for wiring and telecommunications equipment made available pursuant to the Telecommunications Act of 1996. [26] The focus of the legislation is child pornography, obscenity and material deemed "inappropriate" for minors. Several state legislatures are considering similar conditions on funding Internet access in public institutions.[27]

Using government purse strings to pressure local officials to engage in Internet censorship raises troublesome Constitutional questions if the purpose is to suppress certain viewpoints or categories of speech. In a recent case involving federal funding for the arts, the Supreme Court said that "the power to award subsidies" cannot be used to impose a "penalty on disfavored viewpoints"or to "drive 'certain ideas or viewpoints from the marketplace.' "[28] The Court has also

---

[24] Content neutral "time, place and manner" restrictions on chat might be valid in a library if they serve a "substantial governmental interest that would be achieved less effectively absent the regulation." However, the standard does not permit regulations that "may burden substantially more speech than is necessary to further the government's legitimate interests." Banning all chat, even all children's chat, is no more necessary to controlling the behavior of chatters than banning all handbilling is justifiable to eliminating fraud or litter. *Ward v. Rock Against Racism*, 491 U.S. at 799 and note 7.

[25] As of the time of publication, mandatory filtering proposals had been passed by the House and the Senate Commerce Committee. Jeri Clausing, *Filtering Amendment Passes House*, CYBERTIMES (June 19, 1999) <http://www.nytimes.com/library/tech/ 99/06/cyber/articles/19filter.html>; David Hudson, *Children's Internet Protection Act Clears Senate Commerce Committee* (June 24, 1999) <http://www.freedomforum.org/ speech/1999/6/24filter.asp>.

[26] Discounts range from 20% to 90% below commercially available rates, with institutions in the poorest areas receiving the greatest benefits. The program is financed though assessments on users of long distance carriers. It was originally intended to provide subsidies of up to $2.25 billion, but the amount was reduced to $1.3 billion under pressure from the industry. For a current status report on the E-rate, *see* American Library Association, S PECIAL REPORT ON LIBRARY TELECOMMUNICATION DISCOUNTS (June 1999)<http://www.ala.org/washoff/erate.html>.

[27] *See* <http://www.filteringfacts.org> for a summary of state legislation.

[28] In *National Endowment for the Arts v. Finley*, __ U.S. __, 118 S. Ct. 2168 (1998), the Supreme Court upheld the NEA's mandate to consider "general standards of decency" in

---

held that financial benefits generally available to student publications at a public university could not be withheld from a Christian student newspaper because of its message, even though the state's action in denying funding was based on concern about its obligations not to promote or "establish" religion.[29]

Proponents of funding restrictions rely principally on a case in which the Court upheld government funding to provide family planning services, but excluded abortion-related services. [30] The Court held that the "program has not discriminated on the basis of viewpoint; it has merely chosen to fund one activitiy to the exclusion of another." The ruling appears to have little application outside the abortion context, and is distinguishable from a situation in which subsidies intended to facilitate Internet connectivity in public institutions are explicitly conditioned on censorship of certain content.

B. Evaluating the Risks to Minors

The public attention directed at proposals to restrict access to the Internet in public libraries has obscured critical discussion of the nature and extent of the purported dangers of cyberspace. Certainly, the Internet is replete with offensive and disturbing material—racial and ethnic slurs, violent images and sexual material of all kinds. Relationships begun in cyberspace may becoming harassing or may be continued in the real world, where they may pose some risk. Still, a closer look at the evidence suggests that the dangers of unfettered Internet use are greatly exaggerated, particularly where access occurs at a public institution. And as the courts have noted, the benefits of censorship are, at best, "unproven."[31]

---

awarding grants. However, the opinion emphasized that the outcome might well have been different if the decency clause had been a criterion for receipt of funds, rather than one among many factors to be considered.

[29] *Rosenberger v. Rector and Visitors of the University of Virginia*, 515 U.S. 819 (1995)

[30] *Rust v. Sullivan*, 500 U.S. 173 (1991). The Court held that any incidental impact on employee speech was a "consequence of their decision to accept employment," since they remained free to speak about abortion in all other contexts, and patients were free to seek abortion-related information and services elsewhere. For further analysis of *Rust* and *Rosenberger* in the context of current proposals affecting libraries, see the testimony on behalf of People For the American Way in opposition to S. 97 <http://www.pfaw.org/issues/expression/filtering-testimony.html>.

[31] *Reno I*, 521 U.S. at 885.

1. Children and Pornography

Librarians report anecdotally that younger children tend to use the Internet for playing games and return to the same sites rather than simply "surf."[32] Young children also typically require assistance in Internet research, and the guidance of an accompanying adult—a parent or librarian—also minimizes the potential for stumbling across pornographic sites during this activity. Certainly, some children do deliberately seek out sexually explicit material. But after more than two years of aggressive efforts to collect data, the pro-censorship organization Filtering Facts identified only 196 such incidents.[33] Considering that an estimated 344 million children visit public libraries each year[34] and that nearly three-fourths of these libraries offer some form of public Internet access[35] this evidence belies the claim that there is a problem of "epidemic" proportions.

Moreover, the evidence of harm from viewing pornography is, at best, inconclusive. Significantly, none of those advocating restrictions on Internet access in public libraries present any data showing that *occasional* exposure to online pornographic material—whether accidental or deliberate—has adverse effects on either young children or older minors.[36] Based largely on studies of adults, experts on both sides continue to debate the effects of more sustained exposure, but there is no scientific consensus. More than thirty years ago, the

---

[32] Michael Connell, Director, Montclair New Jersey Public Library, personal communication (December 1998)

[33] Filtering Facts, DANGEROUS ACCESS: THE EPIDEMIC OF PORNOGRAPHY IN AMERICA'S PUBLIC LIBRARIES AND THE THREAT TO CHILDREN (February 1999) <http://www.filteringfacts.org/da-main.htm> (hereafter DANGEROUS ACCESS). According to the organization, the average age of children involved in these incidents was 12. A number involved older teens. In addition to these incidents, there are reports of 45 incidents of adults showing pornography to children, a handful of incidents in which patrons allegedly harassed staff and hundred of instances of adults viewing pornography.

[34] The estimate is extrapolated from the number of visitors to public libraries in the United States in fiscal year 1996 (1,013,798,000) and the percentage of children's materials in relation to the total circulation (34 percent). U.S. Department of Education, National Commission of Educational Statistics, PUBLIC LIBRARIES IN THE UNITED STATES: FY 1996 (NCES 1999306) (1999).

[35] 1998 NATIONAL SURVEY, note 17.

[36] The Filtering Facts report does not address the effects on any of the children identified in the cited incidents. Duncan Lindsey, Professor of Social Welfare at UCLA's School of Public Policy and Social Welfare, who is affiliated with the *Child Welfare* web site <http://www.childwelfare.com> and has created "Prowler," second generation filtering software <http://www.webkeys.com> conceded in a personal communication that he was aware of no studies on the effect of exposure to sexually explicit material on the Internet for children of any age. Duncan Lindsey, personal communication (February 1999).

Supreme Court questioned whether material deemed to be "harmful to minors" actually impaired "the ethical and moral development of our youth." Although it upheld the right of the state to regulate, the Court concluded that a causal link had not been demonstrated.[37] In terms of the available research, the situation has not materially changed.

2. Online Stalking and Enticement

The Internet does not create new crimes or criminals, so much as a new environment for criminal acts. That does not make the Internet a uniquely risky environment. In fact, the odds that any particular online conversation will lead to either online harassment or a dangerous real world encounter are relatively small considering that more than 16 million children in the United States—nearly one in four—are online[38] and that millions of communications are occurring at any given moment. And these odds, too, can be decreased significantly if children are educated to follow some basic guidelines about dealing with strangers online, such as not giving out names, phone numbers or other personal information.[39]

Since 1995, the FBI has arrested 270 individuals who stalked children online.[40] For the two-year period ending in December 1998, the National Center for Missing and Exploited Children reported 140 "traveler" cases, in which a child left home or was targeted by an adult to leave home via the Internet. In 74 percent of these cases, the victim was 15 or older,[41] and might have been vulnerable to enticement in any form. Filtering Facts cites only one incident of an online relationship facilitated through public library Internet access and resulting in a real world contact. This incident apparently ended with an arrest.[42]

Significantly, the technology is beginning to address some of these concerns. The Internet is increasingly dangerous for sexual predators as well as those involved in illegal distribution of child pornography and other crimes. For example, the

---

[37] *Ginsberg v. New York*, 390 U.S. 629 (1968).

[38] Cyber Dialogue Research (current as of July 1998) as cited in The Children's Partnership, KIDS AND FAMILIES ONLINE (September 1998). The number is predicted to increase to 20 million children ages 12 and under and 11 million teens by 2002. KIDS AND FAMILIES ONLINE citing Jupiter Communications and NFO Interactive, DECONSTRUCTING THE DIGITAL KID (June 1998).

[39] *See, e.g.*, materials cited at notes 111 and 112.

[40] Sara Sklaroff et. al., *E-mail Nation*, note 34.

[41] National Center for Missing and Exploited Children, ON CHILD SEXUAL EXPLOITATION ON THE INTERNET (December 1998).

[42] DANGEROUS ACCESS, note 71.

with aggressive enforcement efforts by several federal agencies, are increasingly effective in intercepting criminal activities targeting children online.[43] There is also a significant deterrent effect. An anonymous "recovering pedophile" interviewed for Redbook Magazine acknowledged that "on the computer, the search for a victim is an arduous task that's fraught with danger due to the intensity of law enforcement . . ."[44]

Finally, an increasing wealth of material is available to educate parents and others to common warning signs that particular children may be at risk. According to the National Center, those most vulnerable to sexual predators, whether on or off-line, are children who are lonely, suffer from poor self-esteem, and seek attention. Pedophiles provide that attention through an extensive and characteristic "grooming" process, a relationship that typically occurs over a period of weeks and long before any real world encounter. The communications are usually conducted at night, and there is often extensive telephone or mail contact prior to any real world meeting. There are a number of other behavioral indicators that would likely alert parents to potential problems.[45]

3. Media Violence

Until recently, concerns about minors' Internet use have focused primarily on exposure to sexual content.[46] The April 1999 shootings in Littleton, Colorado, however, brought national attention to violence on the Internet and in the media, and have spurred various proposals to label and restrict access to materials with violent content, including books, games and recordings.[47] These measures

---

[43] National Center for Missing and Exploited Children, note 79; FBI web site <http://www.fbi.gov/kids/internet/internet.htm>

[44] Bob Trebilcock, *Child Molesters on the Internet: Are They in Your Home?* REDBOOK (April 1997) Vol. 188, Issue 6 at 100.

[45] Kathy Free, National Center for Missing and Exploited Children, personal communication (January 1999). The FBI's web site <http://www. fbi.gov/kids> also provides a list of cues and suggestions for parents concerned about children's vulnerability to online enticement.

[46] *See* note 7. Significantly, the Annenberg study did not explicitly question parents about violence on the Internet; nor did it analyze media coverage of this issue. Parents were questioned about the relationship between Internet use and "anti-social behavior," but this term is too broad to determine the basis of parents' concern.

[47] These include proposals to prohibit the sale of "violent material" to teenagers, to require a "violence labeling system" for video games, movies and CDS and to prohibit sales to anyone outside the age range identified by the label, and to define violence as a form of obscenity. For a summary of the proposals, *see* People for the American Way Press Release, *Amendments to Juvenile Justice Bill Would Make the First Amendment Another Casualty of Littleton* (June 16, 1999) <http://www.pfaw.org/news/press//

parallel proposed restrictions on minors' access to sexual content, but stand on even shakier constitutional ground. Unlike obscenity and material deemed "harmful to minors," no exceptions apply to material depicting hatred and violence. Even calls to violence fall within the ambit of the First Amendment unless they are both intended to produce and are likely to produce *imminent* lawless action.[48] And efforts to define violence and to limit government regulation to"bad" (i.e.,"excessive" or "gratuitous") violence have been found ambiguous and vague, incapable of objective determination and therefore constitutionally infirm.[49]

The constitutional impediment to restricting minors' access to violent material, however, has not resolved the public debate. The discussion is complicated by a number of factors. First, the causal relationship between violent imagery and violent behavior, like the connection between pornography and sexual acts or attitudes, is a complex one and continues to be hotly debated.[50] Moreover, even

---

Press Release, *Amendments to Juvenile Justice Bill Would Make the First Amendment Another Casualty of Littleton* (June 16, 1999) <http://www.pfaw.org/news/press// show.cgi?article=929570093>. Some, but not all of these proposals have been defeated as this paper goes to press.

[48] *Brandenburg v. Ohio*, 395 U.S. 44 (1969). *But see Planned Parenthood of the Columbia/Willamette, Inc.; et al. v. American Coalition of Life Activists; et al.*, Civil No. 95-1671-J (D.Ore. February 25, 1999)(appeal pending) where the court enjoined "The Nuremberg Files," an anti-abortion website targeting abortion providers, after finding that "a reasonable person would interpret [it] as communicating a serious expression of an intent to inflict or cause serious harm . . ; and the speaker intended that the statement be taken as a threat that would serve to place the listener in fear for his or her personal safety."

[49] For a general discussion of the constitutional principles regarding violent speech, *see* Committee on Communications and Media Law, *Violence in the Media: A Position Paper*, THE RECORD OF THE ASSOCIATION OF THE BAR OF THE CITY OF NEW YORK , V. 21, N. 3 (April 1997) at 273-341 (hereafter *"Violence in the Media*) and Testimony of Robert Corn-Revere before Senate Commerce Committee (May 18, 1999) (TV Violence Hearing), available at <http://www. senate.gov/~commerce/hearings/hearings.html>. Cases challenging regulation of violent content include *Brandenburg* and *Planned Parenthood*, note 86 above; *Interstate Circuit, Inc. v. City of Dallas*, 366 F.2d 590, 598-99 (5th Cir. 1966) *aff'd* 390 U.S. 676 (1968) (declaring unconstitutional statute prohibiting children from viewing movies depicting "brutality" and "criminal violence"); *Video Software Dealers Ass'n v. Webster*, 968 F.2d 684 (8th Cir. 1992) (invalidating Michigan statute prohibiting rental or sale to minors of videos in separate areas of their stores); *Davis-Kidd Booksellers, Inc. v.McWherter*, 866 S.W.2d 520, 530-32 (Tenn. 1993) (law prohibiting distribution of 'excessively violent' materials to minors held unconstitutionally vague).

[50] A 1997 review of the literature concluded "there is no consensus, even among the researchers who have found some correlations, that there is any clear, causal link between

censorship advocates allow that not all violence is harmful; a myriad of contextual factors and cultural values affect the perception and impact of the material.[51] Attempts to distinguish "good" from "bad" violence have been unsuccessful, and most definitions would reach materials as diverse as the Bible, the *Odyssey*, and *Schindler's List*. Finally, data from group studies aside, no researcher has been able to predict what unique combination of images, words and life experiences will trigger an aggressive response—much less a violent act—in any particular individual. Indeed, at this point, there appears to be no common theme that would explain the recent spate of student shootings.[52]

But in any event, broad-based discussions of media violence are not particularly relevant to the Internet, especially in the context of public library access. Other than the news, works of art, and possibly "hate speech" (discussed below) there is relatively little violent imagery on the Internet, and it is unlikely that time-limited Internet access in a library will result in significant exposure to violent material. "First person shooter" video games like Doom and Quake, mentioned repeatedly in connection with the Littleton shootings, cannot be played on the Internet, except in trial versions or with special software which is not typically available in public libraries.

"Hate speech" and bomb making instructions on the Internet pose somewhat different issues. The Internet does facilitate the dissemination of all types of information, including racist and extremist propaganda. This type of material has long been available elsewhere, and the concern that the increased availability of violent material will lead to an increase in violent activity is not supported by the evidence. Interestingly, the number of anti-Semitic incidents reported to the Anti-Defamation League declined steadily between 1994 and 1997—years of

---

media violence and violent behavior." *Violence in the Media,* note 87, at 297. *Compare* Testimony of Leonard Eron, Professor of Psychology and senior research Scientist, Institute for Social Research, University of Michigan before Senate Commerce Committee (May 18, 1999) (TV Violence Hearing) with testimony of Henry Jenkins, Director, Comparative Media Studies Program, Massachusetts Institute of Technology before Senate Commerce Committee (May 4, 1999) (Marketing Violence to Children Hearing), both available at <http://www.senate.gov/~commerce/hearings/hearings.htm>.
[51] Joel Federman (Ed.), NATIONAL TELEVISION VIOLENCE STUDY, Vol. 3 (Executive Summary) (Center for Communication and Social Policy, U.C. Santa Barbara 1997), available at <http://www.ccsp.ucsb.edu/execsum.pdf>.
[52] Bill Dedman, *Secret Service Is Seeking Pattern for School Killers*, NY TIMES (June 21, 1999). Significantly, serious crime by children 12 - 17 is at its lowest rate since 1986. *Upbeat Data on Crime and Youth*, NY TIMES (July 9, 1999).

---

explosive growth in the number of online extremist groups.[53] The survey included any reported overt expression of anti-Semitism such as spray-painted Swastikas and epithets like "dirty Jew," whether or not these could be classified as crimes.[54] On the other side of the debate, insufficient attention has been paid to the fact that the Internet exposes extremist groups to public view and enhances the ability of law enforcement, as well as private groups, to monitor their philosophy, activities and the links between various subgroups.[55]

C. Who Should Decide?

1. The Rights and Responsibilities of Parents

Proposals to restrict public library Internet access are based on a one-size-fits-all approach: all children are equally affected, and potential risks from time-limited library access during the afternoon are treated equally with potential harms from prolonged home-based electronic communications late at night. But as discussed above, there is neither a scientific or social consensus on these issues. An assessment of the risks—and benefits—of different types of Internet use for any particular child is a complex process, one that the government is in no position to undertake. Rather, the determination of whether, where and under what

---

[53] The Simon Wiesenthal Center reported a 300% increase in 1997 in the number of web pages put up by neo-Nazis, white supremacists and other extremists. *See* Jennifer Oldham, *Wiesenthal Center Compiles List of Hate-Based Web Sites* (December 18, 1997) <http://www.wiesenthal.com/itn/times121897.htm>.

[54] Anti-Defamation League, 1998 AUDIT OF ANTI-SEMITIC INCIDENTS <http://www.adl.org/frames/front_98audit.html>. There was a small (slightly more than 2%) increase in incidents in 1998. The Federal Bureau of Alcohol, Tobacco and Firearms reports an increase in 1996 over previous years in the number of bombing incidents attributable to knowledge gained from the Internet. Oral Statement of Special Agent Mark James, ATF Deputy Director of Intelligence Division before Senate Commerce Committee (May 20, 1999) (Protecting Children on the Internet Hearing), available at <http:// www.senate.gov/~commerce/hearings/hearings.htm>. However, in the absence of data on changes, if any, in the total number of incidents during the relevant period and other contextual information, this statistic is difficult to interpret. Many Internet service providers prohibit the posting of bomb-making instructions, and do not link to bomb-making sites. Ruth O'Brien, *Citizens Urge Net Companies to Purge Bomb-Making Sites* (May 20, 1999) <http://www.freedomforum.org/technology/1999/5/20bombsites.asp>.

[55] Private organizations that track extremist activity on and offline include the Southern Poverty Law Center <http://www.splc.org>, The Simon Wiesenthal Center <http://www.wiesenthal.com> and the Anti-Defamation League <http://www.adl.com>.

circumstances a child should be permitted to access the Internet is most appropriately made by parents.[56]

In *Reno I* the Supreme Court reaffirmed its "consistent recognition of the principle that 'the parents' claim to authority in their own household to direct the rearing of their children is basic in the structure of our society.'"[57] Other courts have likewise recognized that different families have different attitudes to sexually explicit material. For example, in a case involving access to a "dial-a-porn" service, a federal circuit court of appeals emphasized "in this respect, the decision a parent must make is comparable to whether to keep sexually explicit books on the shelf or subscribe to adult magazines. No constitutional principle is implicated. The responsibility for making such choices is where our society has traditionally placed it—on the shoulders of the parent."[58]

The Supreme Court has held that the state has an independent interest in the well-being of its youth; that parental guidance cannot always be provided; and that parents are entitled to "the support of laws designed to aid the discharge of [their] responsibilit[ies]."[59] But government regulations should not trump parents' independent determinations to permit their children access to the Internet in public institutions. And governmental actions that burden the exercise of those choices—by requiring parents to sign permission forms or mandating their presence when their children access the Internet–do not avoid the constitutional debate.

---

[56] Some parents are not troubled by sexual material, but are concerned that prolonged computer use will lead to or exacerbate social or psychological problems. The research on the effects of computer use is mixed. A two-year study conducted by researchers at Carnegie-Mellon University concluded that some users experience higher levels of depression and loneliness. Amy Harmon, *Sad, Lonely World Discovered in Cyberspace*, N. Y. TIMES (August 8, 1998). However, the Pew Center for People and the Press did not find these effects. Pew Center for People and the Press, THE INTERNET NEWS AUDIENCE GOES ORDINARY (January 1999)<http://www.people-press.org/tech98sum.htm>. If they exist, these problems would more likely arise from home Internet use as opposed to public library access.

[57] *Reno I*, 521 U.S. at 865, citing *Ginsberg*, 390 U.S. at 639. While the Court refused to address the Government's claim that "the First Amendment does not forbid a blanket prohibition of all 'indecent' and 'patently offensive' messages communicated to a 17-year old - no matter how much value the message may contain and regardless of parental approval, " it seemed especially troubled at the prospect of government interference with a parent's decision, for example, to e-mail birth control information to a teenager.

[58] *Fabulous Associates v. Pennsylvania Public Utility Commission*, 896 F.2d 780, 788 (3rd Cir. 1990).

[59] *Ginsberg v. New York*, 390 U.S. at 639.

---

2. The Independent Rights of Minors

There is a world of difference between a child of six and a sixteen year old, and a rule suitable for one would be indefensible for the other. Children, as they grow and mature, may gain independent constitutional rights to material and Internet communications. Older minors are more likely to use e-mail, to participate in chatrooms and to encounter sexually explicit material through independent Internet research. And, consistent with their own burgeoning sexuality, they are more likely to seek it out. The potential social and educational benefits of their explorations may support a First Amendment right of access, even in the face of parental ignorance or opposition.

The decision in *Reno I* suggests that the Supreme Court may be willing to scrutinize more closely claims about "harm to minors" from sexually explicit material and to evaluate their independent right to gain access to information and ideas. The decision noted that "the strength of the government's interest in protection of minors is not equally strong throughout the broad coverage of this broad statute" and recognized that the statute's ban on "indecent" speech would preclude many "artistic images of educational value" as well as valuable discussion about birth control practices, homosexuality and safer sex.[60] In fact, these discussions are of pressing importance to many teens who rely on information and contacts from the Internet for physical and emotional well being.[61]

A Final Issue: Libraries' Risk of Liability from Hostile Work Environment Claims

Although most discussions of censorship in public institutions focus on potential harm to minors, there is also some concern that the library itself might face liability for declining to filter the Internet—either on the grounds of facilitating minors' access to sexually explicit materials or by creating a sexually hostile work environment. As discussed above, a California Superior Court has held that libraries are not at risk of civil liability for declining to regulate minors' Internet use.[62] Civil liability based on a hostile work environment also appears unlikely.[63]

---

[60] *Reno I*, 521 U.S. at 878-79.
[61] *See* references cited at note 40.
[62] *Kathleen R. v. City of Livermore*, No. V-015266 California Superior Court, Alameda County, Eastern Division. The case, its reasoning and the issue of potential criminal liability are discussed at page 13 and note 58.
[63] For a more complete discussion of this issue, *see,* Memorandum to American Library Association from Jenner and Block *Civil Liability for an Alleged Hostile Work*

A hostile environment is a form of employment discrimination prohibited by federal and most state laws if based on sex, race or other protected classifications. It is conduct that, for both the affected employee and a reasonable person, and considering the "totality of the circumstances," is so "severe or pervasive" as to alter the conditions of employment.[64] Hostile environment claims are most often based on physical actions and conduct coupled with speech—slurs, threats and taunts. Visual materials may also be elements of a hostile work environment, but images and/or words alone are unlikely to be sufficient to sustain such a claim, particularly if the employee can simply avert her eyes or walk away. This is especially true if the display involves protected speech.[65]

The Internet doesn't change the rules. As Filtering Facts claims, a handful of librarians may be troubled by what they see on patrons' computer screens, but this alone does not give rise to institutional liability. A library that has adopted and enforces rules prohibiting unlawful and harassing behavior of all types—on and offline—is unlikely to be at risk.

E. Less Restrictive Alternatives: Solutions At the Local Level

Eighty-five percent of libraries offering public Internet access do not use filtering software,[66] although, in the wake of media attention to the "dark side" of online life, they are facing increasing pressure to restrict children's access.[67] Instead, they are crafting sound and creative solutions, consistent with local needs.

Environment Related to Patron or Employee Internet Use (August 1998) <http://www.ala.org/alaorg/oif/work_jb.html>.

[64] *Harris v. Forklift Systems, Inc.*, 510 U.S. 17, 21 (1993).

[65] In *Stanley v. The Lawson Co*, 1997 WL 835480 (ND Ohio Feb. 26, 1997), cited in the Jenner and Block Memorandum, note 87 above, a convenience store clerk alleged a hostile work environment from the fact that she was required to sell sexually oriented magazines. The court rejected her claims because, among other reasons, removal of the magazines by court order would violate the First Amendment.

[66] 1998 NATIONAL SURVEY, note 17.

[67] A 1997 study by the Urban Libraries Council reported that 60% of the libraries in its sample experienced no pressure to limit Internet access and of those that did experience pressure, 59% characterized it as "low" pressure. National Urban Libraries Council, INTERNET ACCESS AND USE (September 1997). However, according to Jo Rodger, President of the Council, these statistics are no longer valid and media attention to Internet dangers has filtered down to the local level. Jo Rodger, personal communication (April 1999). The shooting incident in Littleton, Colorado has increased interest in filtering, as indicated by mandatory filtering proposals. *See* page 14.

Acceptable Use Policies ("AUPs") have been adopted by an estimated 97 percent of libraries offering public access.[68] Most policies warn that Internet information may be incomplete, inaccurate or offensive and state that parents must assume responsibility for supervising their children's use. Most AUPs explicitly prohibit illegal activity on library workstations, as well as use of the computer for harassment.[69] Time limits on computer use are typical features of almost all library Internet programs,[70] whether or not they are specified in the AUP. Libraries with more than one Internet access outlet are experimenting with reserving terminals for priority uses at certain times of day.[71]

Most libraries also offer Internet training for patrons,[72] and this often includes instruction to help users navigate safely and intelligently through cyberspace. Trained to analyze, evaluate and prioritize different sources of information, librarians are well positioned to serve as guides. "Safe Surfing" or "Internet Drivers Ed" programs, supported by a wealth of valuable material from the American Library Association,[73] as well as government agencies,[74] are valuable both for children and adults. Some libraries are considering requiring such training as a condition of Internet use. Complementing these educational efforts, many libraries (whether or not they have their own World Wide Web pages) have created introductory screens for their users that offer a menu of choices and hyperlinks to recommended sites, arranged by topic and by age level.[75] The

---

[68] 1998 NATIONAL SURVEY, note 17.

[69] A collection of AUPs, current as of 1997, is found at <http://www.ci.oswego.or.edu/library/poli.htm>. The site includes links to the policies of individual libraries, which are more current.

[70] The Urban Libraries Council study, cited at note 105, reports that 90% of the sampled libraries limit use. The average time period is 38 minutes, with 16 to 30 minutes the most frequently cited limit.

[71] These issues are frequent topics of discussion in the public librarians' newsgroup, PUBLIB-NET <http://sunsite.berkeley.edu/PubLib>.

[72] According to the ULC report, 71% offer individual instructions, while 77% provide group instruction.

[73] The American Library Association's publication, A LIBRARIAN'S GUIDE TO CYBERSPACE FOR PARENTS AND KIDS is a key resource, relied on by many libraries. It is distributed in print, with assistance from American Online and is available online <http://www.ala.org/parentspage>. Numerous libraries, such as the New York Public Library, have also developed special screens for children's use. *See* <http://www.nypl.org/branch/kids>.

[74] For example, the FBI site <http://www.fbi.gov> and the Department of Education site <http://www.ed.gov/ pubs/parents/internet> offer educational materials.

[75] *See, e.g.,* the introductory screen of the New York Public Library <http://www.nypl.org>.

---

screens can be developed relatively inexpensively by library personnel based on the preferences and needs of the community, but do not preclude patrons from exploring other areas of cyberspace.

In professional journals and online newsgroups, librarians around the country are considering additional means of encouraging appropriate uses of the Internet, consistent with the character of the library and traditional values of privacy and anonymity: Are privacy screens more trouble than they're worth? Should librarians monitor what patrons are viewing online? If the material is sexually explicit is a shoulder tap necessary or appropriate? Are sign-in policies helpful and, if so, how much information should be collected? As a practical matter, what efforts would be required to enforce parental permissions? Is it possible for librarians to determine which minors might have an independent constitutional right to some material?[76] Can concerns be satisfied if the "default" position is unfiltered access and patrons are free to opt-in for filtering?

In the long-term, the positive experiments in many local libraries, the continuing efforts of librarians to seek better solutions, and the mounting evidence of the inefficiency of filtering[77] may dampen some of the enthusiasm for this approach in public libraries, at least in the United States.[78] In addition, legislation to control spam,[79] to protect privacy and prevent unwanted commercial exploitation

---

[76] *See* discussion at page 21 regarding minors' independent First Amendment rights.

[77] *See* references cited at note 54 above.

[78] In the European Community, however, there remains considerable enthusiasm for filtering. The industry has been encouraged to self-regulate using decentralizing labeling systems that would allow for flexibility to accommodate national, regional, local and personal sensibilities. European Commission, GREEN PAPER ON THE PROTECTION OF MINORS AND HUMAN DIGNITY IN AUDIOVISUAL AND INFORMATION SERVICES <http://www2.echo.lu/legal/en/internet/ gpen-txt.html>. *See also*, Council of the European Union, ACTION PLAN FOR PROMOTING SAFER USE OF THE INTERNET (adopted December 21, 1998) <http://www2.echo.lu/legal/en/internet/comminic.html>. The Yale Law School Information Society Project has a developed an international "best practices model" for industry self-regulation which relies on self-rating and filtering, <http://www.law.yale.edu/infosociety/projects.html#filtering>.

[79] Proposals currently under consideration address issues such as the cost of spam to Internet Service Providers (ISPs) and users, mandatory opt-out measures and false labeling. California treats spam as a form of trespass and enhances the ability of ISPs to establish and enforce their own rules. *See generally*, Jeri Clausing, *More States Consider Restricting Junk E-Mail*, CYBERTIMES (February 11, 1999) <http://www.nytimes.com/library/99/02/cyber/articles/11spam.html>.

---

of children and adults[80] will impact the terms of the censorship debate by addressing these concerns directly.

Still, it is unlikely that the censorship pressures will disappear. New technology is being touted as offering sharper tools for discriminating between so-called "appropriate" and "inappropriate" content and is capable of screening e-mail, chat and other functions.[81] Myriad variations on the filtering theme—filters at some terminals in some locations within the library and not at others—are still under consideration locally and among state and federal legislatures.[82] Similarly, some libraries are continuing to experiment with permutations of the parental permission requirement, including "Smart Cards" coded to indicate parental controls.[83] Each of these approaches requires not only an assessment of the practical impact of the proposal on the library and its staff, but also close analysis under the First Amendment.[84] Moreover, given the uncertain contours of the law, communities must consider whether, as a matter of policy, implementing measures that restrict the free flow of information and ideas is a wise course. A critical factor in the inquiry will be the success of less restrictive alternatives to censorship through education, AUPs and other means.

---

[80] Online privacy and consumer protection are critical issues that are beginning to receive needed attention. In April, 1999, the Federal Trade Commission proposed rules to implement the Children's Online Privacy Protection Act of 1998, Title XIII of the Omnibus Consolidated and Emergency Supplemental Appropriations Act, P.L. 105-277, which prohibits certain unfair and deceptive practices related to the collection of information from and about children under 13. The Act and the proposed regulations are available at <http://www.ftc.gov/privacy>. Legislation has been proposed to protect those not covered byt the Act (*see* H.R. 369, the Children's Privacy Protection and Parental Empowerment Act) and the Administration has announced an initiative to reach potential fraud and abuse in online financial services. *See* <http://www.epic.org/privacy/financial/clinton_remarks_5_99.html>. Also, under pressure from both government and consumers, the industry is stepping up efforts to self-regulate with technology to enable users to set their own privacy boundaries and let sites post privacy policies. Maria Seminerio, *New Cyber Privacy Policy has Powerful Support*, PC WEEK ONLINE (April 6, 1999) <http://www.zdnet.com/pcweek/stories/news/0,4153,1014290,00.html>; *IBM Takes A Stand for Online Privacy Standards*, CYBERTIMES (April 1, 1999).

[81] *See, e.g.*, <http://www.netnanny.com>.

[82] *See* Jeri Clausing, *State Legislators Across U.S. Plan to Take Up Internet Issues*, N. Y. TIMES (January 24, 1999). *See also* note 65.

[83] Ginny McKibben, *Library to Curb Kids' 'Net Scope*, DENVER POST ONLINE (December 30, 1998) <http://www.denverpost.com/news/news1230.htm>.

[84] Karen G. Schneider, author of A PRACTICAL GUIDE TO INTERNET FILTERS (Neal-Schuman Publishers 1997) and a columnist for American Libraries has created a grid showing various filtering options and the pros and cons of each, including potential legal issues. Now somewhat out of date, it nevertheless remains a useful guide and is available at <http://www.bluehighways.com/filters/options.html>.

Conclusion

Computers and the Internet are changing our society in ways we can only begin to imagine. Creating new outlets for expression, expanding the audience for information, and lowering barriers to participation, the technology has the potential to foster free speech, the exchange of ideas, intellectual inquiry, and democracy in new and unique ways. The public library, a place of first and last resort, can play a critical role in that process by offering to all who seek it access to a virtually unlimited world of information, ideas, connections, and conversations.

These changes threaten established communities, structures, and hierarchies. They force us to reexamine our commitment to First Amendment values and to explore constitutional and democratic principles in a new context - one in which the barriers to free speech and inquiry are created, rather than imposed by the limits of technology. Libraries will be the laboratories in which some of the possibilities created by the Internet - for expanded freedom, enhanced education and knowledge, and more inclusive democracy - can be tested and explored.

The participants in these experiments would do well to heed the observation of a federal judge in ruling against censorship of the Internet:

> Indeed, perhaps we do the minors of this country harm if First Amendment protections, which they will with age inherit fully, are chipped away in the name of their protection.[85]

---

[85] *American Civil Liberties Union v. Reno*, 31 F.Supp. 2d at 498.

Additional Resources

Access Denied: The Impact of Internet Filtering Software
on the Lesbian and Gay Community
Gay & Lesbian Alliance Against Defamation
http://www.glaad.org/glaad/access_denied/index.html

This report analyzes the legal, political and social implications of enforced invisibility on the Web. The report also includes a thorough review of the currently available software, ratings systems and search engines, as well as recommendations for industry leaders on how to make the Internet both friendly and fair.

Blacklisted by Cyber Patrol: From Ada to Yoyo
The Censorware Project
http://censorware.org/reports/cyberpatrol/ada-yoyo.html

This report examines some of the thousands of sites that Cyber Patrol blocks in their entirety, against two criteria: first, that blocking should be accurate, and second, that blocking should not be overbroad. It finds that Cyber Patrol blocks a great many sites which do not deserve to be, and that furthermore, looking at past reports of the product's accuracy, fixing these errors is a low priority.

Blocking Software FAQ
Peacefire
http://www.peacefire.org/info/blocking-software-faq.html

Questions and answers about blocking software and its impact on free expression.

*Censorship in a Box: Why Blocking Software
is Wrong for Public Libraries*
American Civil Liberties Union
http://www.aclu.org/issues/cyber/box.html

This special report by the American Civil Liberties Union provides an in-depth look at why mandatory blocking software is both inappropriate and unconstitutional in public libraries.

Censorware Project
http://www.censorware.org/

A group dedicated to exposing the phenomenon of censorware: "software which is designed to prevent another person from sending or receiving information, usually on the web."

Clairview Internet Sheriff: An Independent Review
Electronic Frontiers Australia
http://www.efa.org.au/Publish/report_isheriff.html

In June 1999, the Australian Government enacted Internet censorship legislation requiring Internet Service Providers (ISPs) to block adults' access to particular content on the Internet. This report evaluates one of the country's filtered ISPs in terms of its stated objectives.

Computer Professionals Question Internet Filtering Agreement
Computer Professionals for Social Responsibility
http://www.cpsr.org/dox/issues/filters.html

Brief reaction to industry proposals presented at a White House Summit promoting the use of content rating labels. These labels would be used by browsers and other software to block sites with objectionable content.

Content Rating and Filtering
Electronic Frontiers Australia
http://www.efa.org.au/Issues/Censor/cens2.html

A comprehensive listing of resources on filtering and rating issues from an Australian perspective.

Deja Voodoo: The "X-Stop Files" Revisited.
The Censorware Project
http://censorware.org/reports/xstop/

A study of the "X-Stop" filtering system, which was installed on all computers in the public libraries in Loudoun County, Virginia, before the practice was declared unconstitutional by a federal court.

Encouraging Value Over Filters: A Concise Guide to the "Internet Content Problem" for Parents, Teachers and Netizens Worldwide.
http://members.tripod.com/~rtiess/networth/

A review of alternative approaches to objectionable content that do no require the use of content filters.

Faulty Filters: How Content Filters Block Access to Kid-Friendly Information on the Internet
Electronic Privacy Information Center
http://www2.epic.org/reports/filter-report.html

A report on the impact of software filters on the open exchange of information on the Internet, based on a comparison between 100 searches using a traditional search engine and the same 100 searches using a new search engine that is advertised as the "world's first family-friendly Internet search site."

Filtering FAQ
Computer Professionals for Social Responsibility
http://quark.cpsr.org/~harryh/faq.html

This document attempts to describe the concerns and issues raised by the various types of filtering software. It is hoped that these questions and answers will help parents, libraries, schools, and others understand the software that they may be considering (or using).

Internet Censorship Report: The Challenges for Free Expression Online
Canadian Committee to Protect Journalists
http://www.ccpj.ca/publications/internet/index.html

Reviews the potential impact of software filters on the free exchange of information and ideas over the Internet.

The Internet Filter Assessment Project
http://www.bluehighways.com/tifap/

The Internet Filter Assessment Project ran from April to September, 1997. It was a librarian-led project managed by librarian and author Karen G. Schneider. The purpose of this project was to take a hard look at Internet content filters from a librarian's point of view.

Joint Statement for the Record on "Kids and the Internet:
The Promise and the Perils"
Submitted to the National Commission on Library and Information Science by members of the Internet Free Expression Alliance
http://www.ifea.net/joint_nclis_statement.html

This joint submission argues against the use of filtering and rating systems in public libraries and urges the development of educational programs to teach children "critical thinking skills when using the Internet."

Loudoun County, Virginia Library Filtering Lawsuit
People for the American Way
http://www.pfaw.org/courts/index.shtml#intcensorship

Background information on the litigation that resulted in a judicial decision declaring the use of Internet filters in public libraries unconstitutional. Includes the text of the court decision and selected legal documents.

Nation Trending Toward Do-it-Yourself Censorship
Tony Mauro (published by The Freedom Forum First Amendment Center)
http://www.fac.org/fanews/fan9709/cover.htm

Report on the privatization of censorship following the CDA decision.

The Net Labeling Delusion – Saviour or Devil?
Irene Graham
http://rene.efa.org.au/liberty/label.html

This site offers an alternative resource for information about PICS and PICS facilitated systems. Here you will find reasons for the view that PICS is the devil, rather than our saviour.

Passing Porn, Banning the Bible: N2H2's Bess in Public Schools.
The Censorware Project.
http://censorware.org/reports/bess/

A study of the "Bess" Internet blocking software from N2H2 Inc. finds that the product blocks many innocuous sites, including a version of the Bible compiled by Thomas Jefferson, a site on Darwin and evolution, an issue of Redbook Magazine, and sites dealing with issues as diverse as Serbia, baseball, psychiatry and celibacy.

Peacefire: Youth Alliance Against Internet Censorship
http://www.peacefire.org

Peacefire.org was created in August 1996 to represent the interests of people under 18 in the debate over freedom of speech on the Internet. The Web site and mailing lists are maintained by Bennett Haselton, a mathematics student in Nashville. Peacefire has about 3,300 members on its mailing list as of January 1999; you can join Peacefire and get on the mailing list at no cost. Peacefire also has about 12 staff members that run the organization, and almost all the staff members are teenagers, although some of the older ones are starting to turn 20.

A Practical Guide for Internet Filters
Karen G. Schneider
http://www.bluehighways.com/filters/

Includes product reviews of leading filter products, how filters work, a key features to look for, and configuring filters for most appropriate use in a library environment. Case studies of libraries using filters – and not using filters – will help you decide what your response is for your library, today, and arm you with best current practices to support your decision. One chapter describes The Internet Filter Assessment Project.

Public Interest Principles for Online Filtration,
Ratings and Labelling Systems)
Electronic Frontier Foundation
http://www.eff.org/pub/Censorship/Ratings_filters_labelling/eff_filter.principles

Draft of a policy statement addressing questions such as: Who's watching and recording what? What happens to my personal information when I send it to a filtering site? Who decides whether a site is to be blocked by this filtering software I use?

Ratings Today, Censorship Tomorrow
J. D. Lasica (published by Salon Magazine)
http://www.salonmagazine.com/july97/21st/ratings970731.html

"The Net industry is rushing to embrace ratings systems for the Web. The technology will help parents keep their kids away from porn. It can also help anyone censor anything."

Statement on Internet Filtering
American Library Association, 1997
http://www.ala.org/alaorg/oif/filt_stm.html

"The use in libraries of software filters which block Constitutionally protected speech is inconsistent with the United States Constitution and federal law and may lead to legal exposure for the library and its governing authorities."

To Be Young, Cyber and Free
John Katz (published in The Netizen)
http://www.netizen.com/netizen/97/15/katz4a.html

New media commentator John Katz writes, "Blocking software, not books and ideas, should be banned from libraries and schools."

Tyranny in the Infrastructure
Lawrence Lessig (printed in Wired magazine)
http://www.wired.com/wired/archive/5.07/cyber_rights.html

Law professor Lawrence Lessig reviews the Platform for Internet Content Selection (PICS) filtering proposal and concludes that "PICS is the devil."

X-Rated Ratings?
J.D. Lasica (published by American Journalism Review)
http://ajr.newslink.org/ajrjdl21.html

The Clinton administration and the Internet industry have championed voluntary ratings for Web sites to create a "family-friendly" environment in cyberspace. Their campaign nearly led online news organizations to create a licensing system for Web journalism.